# Bristol 1910–59

KEY Books

AVIATION INDUSTRY SERIES, VOLUME 5

**Front cover image**: A 252 Squadron Beaufighter VI at El Magrun Libya, circa August 1943. (Via *Aeroplane*)

**Back cover image**: Instone Air Line Freighter G-BISU.

**Title page image**: The Shuttleworth Collection's Blenheim V6028 during its brief return to the air in 1987.

**Contents page image**: A Bristol-Prier Monoplane is inspected at Larkhill in 1912 in front of the company sheds, which used the combined titles of two Bristol companies, 'The British and Colonial Aeroplane Company Limited' and 'The Bristol and Colonial Aeroplane Company Limited'. (*Aeroplane*)

Published by Key Books
An imprint of Key Publishing Ltd
PO Box 100
Stamford
Lincs PE9 1XQ

www.keypublishing.com

Original edition published as *Bristol Company Profile 1910–1959* © 2014, edited by Martyn Chorlton.

Unless otherwise stated, all images are from the collection of Martyn Chorlton.

This edition © 2022

ISBN 978 1 80282 379 0

All rights reserved. Reproduction in whole or in part in any form whatsoever or by any means is strictly prohibited without the prior permission of the Publisher.

Typeset by SJmagic DESIGN SERVICES, India.

# Contents

| | |
|---|---|
| Introduction ................................................. 4 | Type 92 .................................................. 80 |
| The Bristol Story ......................................... 5 | Badminton ............................................. 82 |
| Zodiac ..................................................... 12 | Bagshot .................................................. 84 |
| Biplane ('Boxkite') ..................................... 14 | Bulldog .................................................. 86 |
| Bristol Glider ............................................ 16 | Type 101 ................................................ 90 |
| Racing Biplane ......................................... 18 | Type 107 Bullpup .................................... 92 |
| Bristol Monoplane .................................... 20 | Type 109 ................................................ 94 |
| Biplane Type 'T' ....................................... 22 | Type 110A .............................................. 96 |
| Bristol-Prier Monoplanes .......................... 24 | Type 118 and 120 .................................... 98 |
| Gordon England Biplanes ......................... 26 | Type 123 and 133 .................................. 100 |
| Bristol-Coanda Monoplanes ..................... 28 | Type 130 Bombay .................................. 102 |
| Bristol-Burney Flying Boats ...................... 30 | Type 142 .............................................. 106 |
| Bristol-Coanda Two-Seat Biplanes ............. 32 | Type 143 .............................................. 110 |
| Scout Types A to D and S.S.A and S.2A ..... 34 | Type 138 High Altitude Monoplane ......... 112 |
| T.T.A and F.3A ......................................... 36 | Type 146 and 148 .................................. 114 |
| M.1A, M.1B and M.1C Monoplane Scouts .. 38 | Blenheim Mk I, IF, II and Bolingbroke I ... 116 |
| F.2A and F.2B Fighter ............................... 40 | Blenheim IV, IVF and Bolingbroke IV ...... 120 |
| M.R.1 Metal Biplane ................................. 44 | Beaufort ............................................... 122 |
| Scout E and F .......................................... 46 | Beaufighter Mk IF and IC ........................ 124 |
| Braemar, Pullman and Tramp .................... 48 | Beaufighter Mk II, IIF and V .................... 126 |
| F.2C Badger I, II and X ............................. 50 | Bisley Mk I and Blenheim V .................... 128 |
| Tourer and Coupé .................................... 52 | Beaufighter Mk VI, VIC and VIF .............. 130 |
| Babe ....................................................... 54 | Beaufighter Mk X ................................... 132 |
| Bullet ..................................................... 56 | Buckingham and Buckmaster .................. 134 |
| Seely ...................................................... 58 | Beaufighter Mk 21 ................................. 138 |
| Ten-Seater and Brandon ........................... 60 | Brigand ................................................. 140 |
| Bullfinch ................................................. 62 | Type 170 Freighter and Wayfarer ............ 142 |
| M.1D ...................................................... 64 | Type 171 and Sycamore ......................... 144 |
| Racer ...................................................... 66 | Type 167 Brabazon Mk 1 ........................ 146 |
| Taxiplane and Primary Trainer ................... 68 | Type 173 and Belvedere ......................... 148 |
| Bloodhound ............................................ 70 | Britannia 100 ........................................ 152 |
| Jupiter-Fighter and Advanced Trainers ...... 72 | Britannia 300 ........................................ 154 |
| Brownie .................................................. 74 | Britannia C Mk 1 and C Mk 2 .................. 156 |
| Berkeley .................................................. 76 | Type 188 .............................................. 158 |
| Boarhound and Beaver ............................. 78 | |

# Introduction

While not the first aircraft manufacturer in Britain, Bristol had the distinct advantage of being created by a well-established businessman, rather than an enthusiastic aviator, by the name of Sir George White. Born in Cotham, Bristol in 1854, White's business experience began when he was a junior clerk working for a group of solicitors. It was while working on bankruptcy cases that White learned how a business should be run and this knowledge stood him in good stead. In 1874, White was appointed as Company Secretary of the newly formed Bristol Tramway Company, rising to Chairman in 1900, a position that he held until his death in 1916.

By the time Sir George White began showing an interest in aviation, he was a highly respected businessman who could clearly see commercial potential in flying machines in civilian and military hands. It was during a visit to France in 1909 that he met many leading aviators, including aviation pioneer Wilbur Wright, who inspired him to establish an aircraft factory in his home city of Bristol. This new aviation venture began business with an initial investment of £25,000, which compared favourably with that of the fledgling Short Brothers and Handley Page companies, which began with comparatively conservative investments of £600 and £500 respectively.

Bristol grew rapidly from a few hangars at the influential Larkhill, Wiltshire, to a new site at Filton – which is the company's spiritual home – and, up until 2012, was a key aviation design, development and manufacturing location in Britain. In recognition of this, the new Aerospace Bristol, a heritage museum run by Bristol Aero Collection Trust, with Concorde as its centrepiece, was established at Filton, bolstered by the Bristol Aero Collection, which has moved in from Kemble. The site for the new centre was donated by BAE Systems which, along with Rolls-Royce and Airbus, pledged large sums of money to get this important venture established.

Thanks to the many talented designers, engineers, test pilots and vision of Sir George more than a century ago, Bristol has made its mark on the aviation industry with revolutionary aircraft that have broken records along the way. Both military and civilian aircraft and the engines – piston, turboprop and jet – have benefited from the standard in engineering excellence set on the hallowed ground of Filton.

**The first production Brigand was TF Mk 1, RH742, which enjoyed a lengthy career (for a Brigand), serving with the Empire Central Flying School (ECFS), Aeroplane and Armament Experimental Establishment (A&AEE) and the Armoured Trials and Development Unit (ATDU).** (*Aeroplane*)

# The Bristol Story

## Gaining a foothold

Sir George White was a businessman with many interests, including being chairman of the Bristol Tramway and Carriage Company. He was intrigued by the flights made by the Wright brothers and by other aviation pioneers in Britain and France. White could see the potential of aviation and decided to capitalise on this fast-growing sector by forming four companies on 19 February 1910: The Bristol Aeroplane Company Ltd; The Bristol Aviation Company Ltd; The British Colonial Aeroplane Company Ltd; and The British Colonial Aviation Company Ltd.

He chose to trade using the third title registered and with the aforementioned working capital of £25,000 raised between himself, his brother Samuel and his son Stanley White. Sir George established the business as a separate company from the Bristol Tramway Company, because he considered that such a venture would be viewed as too risky by many shareholders and that public subscriptions for an aviation venture would be regarded with deep suspicion. Sir George, his brother and son were directors with Sir George as Chairman.

On 28 February 1910, the first meeting of the new company was held at the registered office in Clare Street, Bristol. Henry White Smith and Sydney Smith, Sir George's nephews, were appointed secretary and manager, respectively, and Émile Stern was appointed company agent in France. This was important, as the British Colonial Aeroplane Company had reached and signed an agreement to manufacture aircraft designed by the Société Zodiac, a recently established French aerospace company. In 1910, aircraft design was more advanced in France than in Britain and – as no one connected with the new enterprise knew anything about aeroplanes – made commercial sense.

Sydney Smith and Herbert Thomas, Sir George's younger nephew, went to Paris to examine the products of Société Zodiac and to arrange for one of that company's aircraft to be shown at the Aero Exhibition at Olympia, London, in March. This Zodiac biplane, designed by Gabriel Voisin, duly arrived at the premises White had rented at Filton, near Bristol, from the Bristol Tramways Corporation. Following the show at Olympia, the aircraft was moved by road to Brooklands, Surrey, where the company had taken a shed near the flying area. Brooklands had been built as a race and test track for British automobile manufacturers, but the large, uncluttered central area had attracted several pioneer aviators such as AV Roe and Thomas Sopwith among others.

With the assistance of a French engineer from Société Zodiac, the biplane was erected and made ready for flight. Unfortunately, it refused to leave the ground and nothing pilot Maurice Edmond could do would make it fly. It managed a brief hop before it was abandoned, likewise the five other similar Zodiac machines being built at Filton. The directors of the British and Colonial Aircraft Company sued Société Zodiac for compensation and for supplying an aircraft that did not fly. In the event, the French firm settled with a payment of 15,000 francs and the contract between the two companies was cancelled.

Having lost time with the Zodiac design, the works manager of British and Colonial, George Challenger, had taken the advice of the French pilot Maurice Edmond, who had been sent to fly the Zodiac, and started manufacturing a biplane to his own design, which was largely based on the published designs of the British-French aviators, the Farman brothers. Stern had secured the British Empire agency rights for the French Gnome engine and a 50hp example was installed in Challenger's aircraft. As the design was Farman-based, it was natural that the Farman brothers were unhappy that several of their patents had been infringed. However, they did not take action and remained on good terms with the Bristol-based company and its personnel. Work on the first of two aircraft – known erroneously as Boxkites – was completed by June 1910 and it was taken to Larkhill for test flying. The directors of British and Colonial had leased a site and the flying rights to 2,000 acres of land at Larkhill on Salisbury Plain from the War Office. With a flying school established at Brooklands and another at Larkhill, there was no shortage of pupils and in time these flying schools came to be regarded as some of the best in the world. By 1914, 308 of the 664 Royal Aero Club certificates issued to date had been received by the two schools.

**The majestic Brabazon airliner with cutting-edge late 1940s/1950s design attempted to provide a passenger service for a pre-war clientele. Today's aircraft of this size today carry three times the number of passengers that the Brabazon was designed to take.**

Filton aerodrome during the early 1930s, looking west-northwest. The airfield progressively expanded westwards. The World War One hangars and buildings were systematically replaced, while the main sheds in the upper right of this photograph have been preserved.

*Above left*: Bristol's long-serving designer, Frank Barnwell, whose life was cut short in an aircraft accident on 2 August 1938.

*Above right*: Sqn Ldr Swain being assisted into his high-altitude pressure helmet by staff of the Royal Aircraft Establishment (RAE) on 10 September 1936 for a test flight in the Bristol Type 138. He took the altitude record eight days later.

## Bristol to the forefront

While the Bristol Boxkite was a good aircraft, it was not capable of further development and other designs were being developed by the new team at Filton. Challenger left to join Vickers and in his place Henri Coanda was taken on as chief designer. However, it was after Coanda left and Frank Barnwell took over the post that aircraft from the Bristol Aircraft Company, as it was referred to, came to the forefront. Under Barnwell's leadership, aircraft such as the Bristol Monoplane, Bristol Fighter and Bristol Bulldog entered Royal Flying Corps (RFC) and Royal Air Force (RAF) service.

In 1920, the British and Colonial Aircraft Corporation was liquidated and its assets transferred to the Bristol Aeroplane Company Ltd, after which business continued, and work concentrated on military aeroplanes. Archibald Russell (later Sir Archibald) joined the Bristol Tramway and Carriage Company in 1924 as an assistant fitter; a year later he transferred to the drawing office of the Bristol Aeroplane Company where he worked on more than 30 of the aircraft designs that originated at Filton.

During World War Two, Bristol manufactured the vital Blenheim and Beaufighter aircraft and had plans for post-war developments of the latter. The Buckingham and Buckmaster evolved from the Beaufighter, both of which were intended for wartime service. Finally, the Brigand filled an RAF operational need in the Middle and Far East.

It was during 1942 that Bristol reached its peak employment with 52,095 personnel working in all company works including shadow factories at Accrington in Lancashire, and Weston-super-Mare. A further 100 dispersal sites also contributed to the Bristol machine including more obscure locations such as Wells Prison, Highbridge Cheese Stores, a few rooms in Loxton Rectory and even under a railway arch in Worcester. Engine repair shops sprang up in the most diverse of locations including a tobacco bonded store. Spar assembly made use of a bus station, while gun turrets were manufactured in a chocolate factory, drawing offices were located in hotel rooms and at least one component store was to be found a home in a cider factory.

*Above*: The Type 133 was a typical result of the many new specifications issued by the Air Ministry during the 1930s.

*Left*: The colossal 8-acre Assembly Hall takes shape behind the equally huge part-built Brabazon airliner in 1948.

## Bristol Helicopter Division

Another arm to the Bristol story was the establishment of a Helicopter Department in 1944 with a design team led by Raoul Hafner. His first design was the Type 171, named the Sycamore in military service, which achieved reasonable success. In total, 181 were built. The more ambitious and technologically challenging tandem-rotor Type 171 followed, but the machine failed to stir civilian interest, though it did enter service with the RAF in small numbers as the Belvedere.

Hafner's team was bursting with ideas by the 1950s, all of which were never destined to leave the drawing board. These included the Type 181 with 100ft fuselage, 72ft-diameter rotor blades and the ability to carry up to 80 passengers. The Type 194 was the only project that came close to reaching prototype stage; this helicopter was to be powered by four 1,175shp Gnome engines. However, by 1960, the government had put pressure on all Britain's potential helicopter manufacturers and, along with Fairey and Saunders-Roe, Bristol Helicopters was merged into Westland Helicopters. All of the expertise was quickly re-employed to produce the Westland Westminster and Fairey/Westland Rotodyne and the potentially commercially viable Type 194 was abandoned.

## The influence of Lord Brabazon

In 1942, with the war at its height, aircraft construction in Britain was concentrated on fighters and heavy bombers, leaving the production of transport aircraft to the United States. This would have left Britain with little experience in transport aircraft construction at the end of the war so, in 1943, a committee under Lord JTC Moore-Brabazon, investigated the future of the British civilian airliner market. The Brabazon Committee called for several different aircraft to be developed to specifications proposed to fulfil Britain's civilian aviation needs.

Bristol won the Type I and Type III contracts, delivering its Type I design, the Bristol Brabazon, in 1949. The requirement for the 1946 British Overseas Airways Corporation (BOAC) Medium Range Empire (MRE) Requirements coincided with the Type III, which called for a long-range airliner in the 100,000lb class powered with four piston engines. The result was the Britannia airliner, Britain's first to be powered by turboprops; the lack of sound gave this wonderful aircraft the affectionate nickname the 'Whispering Giant'.

In the meantime, Filton saw another dramatic expansion period, including a new design office and an impressive eight-acre Assembly Hall, built in 1947 for the production of the Brabazon. Built under the direction of civil engineer TP O'Sullivan, the doors on this vast creation were the largest in the world and it has become one of Bristol's landmarks over the years. As a result of the Brabazon, Filton also gained a new, longer and stronger runway, an extension that resulted in the part-demolition of a hamlet at Charlton.

The Britannia never fully realised its full potential from a sales point of view but of the 85 built, many gave good service into the late 1970s and 1980s, especially those aircraft sold by the RAF because of defence cuts. Not covered in this publication are the licence-built Canadair variants made up of the CL-44/CC-106 Yukon and CL-28/CP-107 Argus, of which 37 of the former and 33 of the latter were built.

Bristol, along with many other aircraft manufacturers, began a series of studies into supersonic transport aircraft prompted by the formation of the Supersonic Transport Advisory Committee (part of the Ministry of Aviation), which was formed in 1958. The first Bristol proposal was the Type 198, which was initially a Mach 1.3 design but, once the wing was changed to a slim delta and the engines were mounted underneath in pods, it was clearly capable of Mach 2.2 if powered by six

**Long-serving Bristol chief test pilot Cyril Uwins (right) hands over the reins to 'Bill' Pegg in 1947, with a Blenheim Mk I in the background.**

Olympus turbojets (Mach 2 represents twice the speed of sound.). A Mach 3 version, the Type 213, was abandoned until a re-designed, slightly smaller Type 223 version was seen as the way forward. Coincidentally, across the Channel, Sud Aviation at Toulouse had designed its own Super-Caravelle, which looked very similar to the Type 223. As a result, an Anglo-French agreement was signed in 1962 and work began on the Mach 2.2 airliner, later named Concorde. Subsequently, Filton would become the home of the all British-built Concordes and it was from there that 002 made its maiden flight on 9 April 1969. Appropriately, ex-British Airways Concorde G-BOAF made its final flight to Filton on 26 November 2003, where it remains a popular attraction.

## Industry reorganisation

One commercial aircraft that was a quiet success for Bristol during the immediate post-war period was the Type 170 Freighter; it provided operators with a rugged reliable load carrier. In total, 214 were built, with a number serving into the 1980s. The Freighter/Wayfarer and Britannia carried Bristol through the late 1940s and 1950s, leaving Bristol in a strong financial position by the time the company was divided into three different companies. In January 1956, a reorganisation of the company's three divisions, the Aircraft, Aero-Engine and Car Divisions, saw them re-emerge as Bristol Aircraft Ltd, Bristol Aero-Engines Ltd and Bristol Cars Ltd – all three were under the total ownership of the Bristol Aeroplane Company Ltd. Bristol Air Ltd's facilities would provide the main contribution to the British Aircraft Corporation (BAC), which was formed in June 1960. BAC was effectively a pooling of aviation interests and resources, made up of Bristol, Vickers Ltd, the English Electric Company and later Hunting Aircraft Ltd. On 28 December 1968, BAC (Operating) Ltd was created, which rebranded Bristol Aircraft Ltd to the Filton Division.

**Originally built as the Fairey F.D.2, WG774 was redesigned at Filton by Bristol engineers and renamed the British Aircraft Corporation (BAC, aka Bristol) 221. First flown in 1964, the 221 was used for Concorde development until 1973 and today is preserved in the Fleet Air Arm (FAA) Museum alongside Concorde G-BSST, the last example to fly from Filton.**

Bristol had an incredible record for aircraft production; 22,470 aircraft of 85 different designs were manufactured between February 1910 and June 1960, 15,750 in the company's own works and shadow factories, and 8,320 under license in Britain and overseas. A further 1,600 were built on Bristol premises but were designed by an external company.

On 14 April 2011, BAE Systems, announced that Filton would be closed by late 2012. True to its word, the airfield shut operations on December 21 and ten days later officially closed.

*Right*: Bristol-built 783 Bloodhound Mk I and Mk II missiles remained one of the UK's main air defence weapons until 1991. This example is a Mk I at North Coates in Lincolnshire.

*Below*: It was from the hands of Bristol designers that the Type 223 was penned. Within a decade, the result, Concorde, would be lifting from Filton's runway.

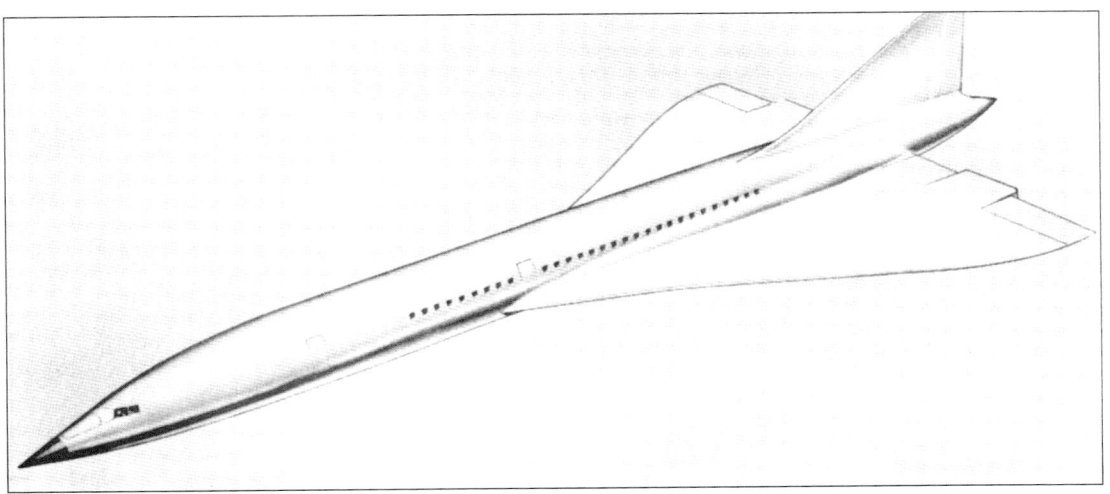

# Zodiac

## Development
In 1907, Gabriel and Charles Voisin produced a new 'boxkite' design in which Henri Farman flew a one kilometre closed course to win a prize of 50,000 francs. The achievement pushed the Voisins to the forefront of aircraft design and they were embraced by the Société Zodiac of Paris.

At the same time, Sir George White was on the hunt for an aircraft that could be manufactured at Filton and, after consulting with Émile Stern, the Zodiac – the boxkite developed by the Voisin brothers, was recommended. It was quickly imported and placed on the newly formed Bristol and Colonial Aeroplane Company's stand at the Aero Show at Olympia in March 1910.

## Design
In keeping with most early Voisin-type biplanes, the Zodiac featured a single elevator in front of the aircraft, a biplane tail mounted on four booms and an engine mounted on the lower wing driving a two-blade propeller behind the trailing edge. A single vertical rudder was positioned between the tailplanes, and surfaces were fixed to the outer mainplane struts in order to reduce sideslip in a turn. Both upper and lower mainplanes and tailplanes were un-cambered and fabric covered. Ailerons were only fitted to the lower wing. The latter were linked to the rudder, which was controlled by a handwheel that moved fore and aft for elevator control.

The undercarriage consisted of a pair of skids with two wheels mounted on each. All in all, the workmanship of the Zodiac was superb, although its flying qualities were lacking.

## Service
Following Olympia, the Zodiac was returned to Filton in preparation for test flying on 30 April, to be carried out by Belgian pilot, Arthur Duray. Unfortunately, Duray met with an accident in France and later the Zodiac headed for Brooklands. Arriving on May 10, the aircraft was erected in the 'Bristol' shed by Sydney Smith and several assistants.

The aircraft proved to be underpowered and, in the hands of Maurice Edmond, refused to fly. The aircraft's wings were replaced with a set of increased camber and on 28 May, Edmond managed a single hop. With low expectations, Edmond tried again on 15 June, but the undercarriage was damaged in the process. With little trouble, Edmond convinced Sydney Smith that a Henri Farman-type design would be more suitable and, as a result, five Bristol Zodiacs already under construction at Filton were scrapped and the licence was cancelled.

## Production

Six aircraft, No. 1 to 6, built by Bristol and Colonial Aircraft Co Ltd under licence from Société Zodiac, Paris, were planned, but only one was assembled.

| Technical data – Zodiac 52B | |
|---|---|
| ENGINE | One 50hp Darracq |
| WINGSPAN | 33ft 3in |
| LENGTH | 39ft 3in |
| HEIGHT | 10ft 2in |
| WING AREA | (Total): 525sq ft |
| SPEED | 35mph |
| ACCOMMODATION | One pilot and passenger |

The hastily assembled Bristol Zodiac biplane at the Aero Show, Olympia, in March 1910. Delivered in crates just before the show, the aircraft's 50hp Darracq engine was supplied without any means of bolting it to the aircraft. Engineer Charles Briginshaw had to manufacture clamps that fitted around the crankcase in order to mount it to the structure.

# Biplane ('Boxkite')

## Development
The first aircraft to be built from scratch by Bristol was also one of the first machines in Britain to be built in substantial numbers. There was no attempt to hide the fact that the 1910 Biplane (only later dubbed the 'Boxkite') was a copy of the Farman III pusher biplane (built in France in 1909). At that time, the build quality of French aircraft was desirable, and so the Bristol Biplane was put together with more refined metal components, including steel clips and cast aluminium strut sockets. These 'improvements' were more than enough to have a patent infringement claim placed by the solicitors of Farman Frères thrown out of court.

## Design
The first pair of Boxkites was produced from plans drawn by works manager and engineer George Challenger in June 1910, immediately after the failure of the Zodiac. These early aircraft had rear elevators with straight trailing edges. The first aircraft built, No. 7 was fitted with a 50hp Grégoire four-cylinder engine, while the second aircraft, No. 8, had a 50hp E.N.V. eight-cylinder powerplant. The Grégoire proved to be underpowered but the addition of one of the first 50hp Gnome engines to be imported into the country solved the problem and would subsequently become the Boxkite's standard powerplant.

## Service
Boxkite No. 7 was transported to Larkhill, on 29 July 1910 and assembled overnight in preparation for its maiden flight the following day. In front of several spectators who were expecting little more than a short hop, Maurice Edmond took off with ease and, after reaching a respectable height of 150ft, landed without incident. The first two aircraft were then sent to Lanark to compete in a six-day aviation meeting on 6 August, but only No. 7 took part.

Later allocated to the fledgling flying schools at Brooklands and Larkhill, production began to gain momentum by the end of 1910. Four aircraft were shipped in pairs for Missions to Australia and India, arriving in December. During the Australian Mission, one of these aircraft, No. 10, flown by Hammond, managed 72 flights covering a distance of 765 miles between January and May 1911, all without any mechanical adjustment.

Orders were received from around the world, beginning with the Russian government, which ordered eight Boxkites, all of which were delivered to St Petersburg in April 1911. The War Office placed its first order for four aircraft in March 1911 to equip No. 2 (Aeroplane) Company of the British Army's Air Battalion, which was formed the following month. The Royal Naval Air Service (RNAS) also operated the type for training duties at Eastbourne, Eastchurch, Chingford and Hendon.

## Production
A total of 78 Boxkites were built by the Bristol and Colonial Aircraft Co Ltd, including two Standard aircraft, 60 Extended (Military), one Racer No. 44, and one Voisin No. 69. All but six Boxkites were built at Filton; the remainder from the Bristol Tramway works at Brislington.

# Biplane ('Boxkite')

| | |
|---|---|
| **Technical data – Boxkite Standard, Extended (Military), Racer No. 44 and Voisin No. 69** | |
| ENGINE | One 50hp Grégoire, 50/60hp E.N.V, 50hp Gnome, 60hp Renault or 70hp Gnome |
| WINGSPAN | (Standard) 34ft 6in; (Mil) 47ft 8in or 46ft 6in; (Racer) 35ft; (Voisin) 32ft 8in |
| LENGTH | (Standard and Mil) 38ft 6in; (Racer) 38ft; (Voisin) 30ft 9in |
| HEIGHT | (Standard, Mil and Racer) 11ft 10in; (Voisin) 9ft 6in |
| WING AREA | (Standard) 457sq ft; (Mil) 517sq ft; (Racer) 350sq ft; (Voisin) 420sq ft |
| EMPTY WEIGHT | (Standard, Racer and Voisin) 800lb; (Mil) 900lb |
| ALL-UP WEIGHT | (Standard) 1,050lb; (Mil) 1,150lb; (Racer and Voisin) 1,000lb |
| SPEED | (Standard and Mil) 40mph; (Racer and Voisin) 50mph |
| ACCOMMODATION | (Standard, Mil and Voisin) two; (Racer) one |

Bristol Biplane ('Boxkite') No. 12A, one of 16 'Standard' variants fitted with a 50hp Gnome engine. This aircraft, along with No. 9, took part in military manoeuvres in India in January 1911.

# Bristol Glider

## Development
Following the election of Sir George White to president of the Bristol and West of England Aero Club at Keynsham, Somerset, in October 1910, a glider was commissioned as a gift to the club. With a thriving membership of 75, the addition of this aircraft to the club's inventory was greatly appreciated.

## Design
Designed by George Challenger, the aircraft, simply known as the Bristol Glider, was of a sturdy, purposeful design. Able to carry two persons aloft, the intention was to mount a 30hp engine at a later stage. With double-surface mainplanes and tailplane, the glider had ailerons fitted only to the upper mainplane for lateral control and the elevators, located forward and aft, were coupled to control pitch. A pair of small rudders was mounted on the rear tail-booms forward of the tailplane, while the foreplane was positioned on wire-braced wooden booms. The latter carried the undercarriage, which were a pair of long skids with small wheels.

The sole Bristol Glider in October 1910.

## Service

The maiden flight of the Bristol Glider took off from Keynsham on 17 December 1910 in the hands of George Challenger. The glider was hand-towed into the air down a slope using ropes attached to the wing-tips. Recovery back up the slope was aided by a twin-wheeled dolly.

The sole Bristol Glider was damaged in February 1911, but the cost of the repairs, amounting to 12 shillings 6 pence, was covered by Bristol. A more serious accident on 4 September 1911 cost £30 to repair.

The idea of fitting a 30hp appears not to have come to fruition.

| Technical data – Bristol Glider | |
|---|---|
| ENGINE | Provision for a 30hp engine |
| WINGSPAN | 32ft 4in |
| LENGTH | 33ft 10in |
| HEIGHT | 6ft 8in |

# Racing Biplane

## Development
Also referred to as the 'Racer', the Bristol Racing Biplane (No. 33) was a single-seat biplane designed by Robert Grandseigne and Léon Versepuy under the guidance of George Challenger. Built during the winter of 1910 and 1911, the Racer was an attempt to produce an aircraft with the performance of a monoplane and the structural strength of a biplane.

## Design
A design with many unusual features, the Racing Biplane's wings were double-surfaced and with an unequal span, the upper being inversely tapered. Each wing was constructed around a single tubular spar made of steel. Lateral control was achieved by warping and the wings could be folded for storage. The composite steel tube and wood fuselage had a rectangular-shaped cross-section and was completely fabric-covered.

Power was provided by a 50hp Gnome engine, which was mounted on double bearers, fully enclosed by an aluminium cowl and drove a four-blade wooden propeller. The undercarriage was also made of steel tube and was attached to the lower longerons. Two wheels were mounted on a rubber-sprung

axle, which was stabilised by a pair of telescopic struts attached to the upper longeron. The novel undercarriage featured a pair of main skids that extended rearwards and acted as brakes on landing. The Racing Biplane had a flexible tail skid.

## Service

On paper, the sole Racing Biplane looked a winner and, even in the flesh, the little aircraft looked promising. It received a great deal of attention after being displayed at Olympia and expectations were high. However, in April 1911, on its first attempt to become airborne, the Racing Biplane overturned on take-off at Larkhill and was wrecked.

| Technical data – Racing Biplane | |
|---|---|
| ENGINE | One 50hp Gnome |
| WINGSPAN | 27ft |
| LENGTH | 25ft |
| WING AREA | 210sq ft |
| EMPTY WEIGHT | 570lb |
| SPEED | 55mph (estimated) |
| ACCOMMODATION | One |

The Bristol Racing Biplane, No. 33, also known as 'The Racer', was wrecked on its first attempted flight at Larkhill, Wiltshire, in April 1911.

# Bristol Monoplane

## Development
Combining the best features of the French-built Bleriot and Antoinette monoplanes, the Bristol Monoplane was the first of its kind to be built by the company.

## Design
Designed by George Challenger and Archibald Low, the Bristol Monoplane unashamedly made full use of two French designs; the warping wing of the Bleriot and the triangular cross-section fuselage of the Antoinette. Power was provided by a 50hp Gnome driving a twin-blade propeller mounted on a steel frame. The straightforward undercarriage proved to be a benchmark design arrangement with a pair of twin main wheels with central skid and a long tail skid. This configuration was later referred to as the 'conventional landing gear' or, in modern terms, a 'tail-dragger' arrangement. The Bristol design preceded the more famous Avro 504, which utilized the same undercarriage design with colossal success.

## Service
With plans for full-scale production in place, the first two Bristol Monoplanes, No. 35 and 36, were completed in February 1911. No. 35 was sent to Larkhill for 'preliminary testing', although it's not entirely clear whether that actually included 'flight testing'. It was then returned to Filton in preparation for display at Olympia in March, where it received significant attention and appreciation.

The second Monoplane, No. 36, was prepared for a similar event in St Petersburg and was displayed from April 23 to 30. In the meantime, No. 35 was prepared for 'flight testing' at Larkhill in May. This was carried out by Léon Versepuy, but the Monoplane failed to take-off and was subsequently damaged. No attempt was made to repair the aircraft and as a result all thoughts of mass-production were diverted to the next design.

## Production

Two aircraft were built, No. 35 and No. 36.

| Technical data – Bristol Monoplane | |
|---|---|
| ENGINE | One 50hp Gnome |
| WINGSPAN | 33ft 6in |
| LENGTH | 31ft 6in |
| HEIGHT | 6ft 8in |
| WING AREA | 215sq ft |
| EMPTY WEIGHT | 580lb |
| ALL-UP WEIGHT | 760lb |
| SPEED | 55mph (Estimated) |
| ACCOMMODATION | One |

**Bristol Monoplane, No. 35 at Larkhill in March 1911 during preliminary testing.**

# Biplane Type 'T'

## Development
Designed by George Challenger for the use of racing pilot Maurice Tabuteau, the Bristol Biplane Type 'T' drew heavily on the experience gained when developing the Boxkite and the advice given by Captain Dickson, resulting in the aircraft sometimes being referred to as the 'Challenger-Dickson' biplane.

## Design
The first of the Type 'T's, serialled No. 45, was a more compact version of the Farman MF.7 Longhorn complete with long upswept skids. Power was provided by a 70hp Gnome Gamma rotary mounted on the rear of a rectangular nacelle, which contained both the petrol and oil tanks. The forward section of the same nacelle contained the pilot who was equipped with a similar push-pull handwheel control to that installed in the Zodiac. A forward elevator was installed at the apex of four forward booms while a single tailplane, twin rudders and elevator were mounted at the rear of four more booms, aft of the engine.

## Service
Designed for cross-country racing, No. 45 was one of 38 aircraft entered for the Circuit de l'Europe air race in 1911. Flown by test pilot Tabuteau, the challenging course covered 1,025 miles travelling from Paris, via Liége, Spa, Venlo, Utrecht, Breda, Brussels, Roubaix, Calais, Dover, Shoreham, Hendon, Dover, Calais and finally back to Paris. The Type 'T' was one of only nine aircraft to complete the race.

    A further four Type 'T's serialled No. 51 to 54 were built for the 1911 Daily Mail Circuit of Britain Air Race. They featured subtle modifications over No. 45 such as a slightly different nacelle and repositioned rudders. No. 51 was entered into the race by pioneer aviator Graham Gilmour but had to be withdrawn after he had his licence suspended because of dangerous flying over the Henley Regatta. No. 52 was flown by Collyns Pizey, who crash landed near Melton Mowbray, while No. 53, flown by Gordon Withdraw, did not fly due to engine problems. No. 54 was powered by a 60hp Renault and flown by Howard Pixton, but this aircraft force landed near Harrogate and never finished. Tabuteau also entered No. 45 and also failed to finish.

    After the *Daily Mail* race, No. 51 was refitted with a 50hp Gnome engine and was sold to pilot Gerald Napier. It crashed at Brooklands on 2 August 1911, killing Napier. No further flights would be made by Type 'T's.

## Production
Six Type 'T's were built, serialled No. 45, 51 to 54 and 78; the latter was installed with a 100hp Gnome but never flew.

## Biplane Type 'T'

| Technical data – Biplane Type 'T' | |
|---|---|
| ENGINE | One 60hp Renault, one 70hp Gnome or one 100hp Gnome |
| WINGSPAN | 35ft |
| WING AREA | 350sq ft |
| EMPTY WEIGHT | 800lb |
| ALL-UP WEIGHT | 1,000lb |
| SPEED | 58mph |
| ACCOMMODATION | One |

Bristol Type T, No. 52, with Flt Lt Collyns Pizey at the controls, warms through its 70hp Gnome engine at Larkhill in June 1911.

# Bristol-Prier Monoplanes

## Development
The chief instructor of the Blériot School, Pierre Prier, had made quite a name for himself in April 1911 when he became the first man to fly non-stop from London to Paris. An experienced pilot and qualified engineer, Prier was also enthusiastic about designing his own aircraft. Following the departure of George Challenger and Archibald Low to Vickers, Prier was invited to join Bristol in June 1911.

## Design
Of similar lines to the Blériot XI, Prier designed five different monoplanes; two were single-seaters, named the P-1 and 'single seat school' powered by a range of engines including the 35hp Anzani, 40hp Isaacson, 40hp Clément-Bayard and the 50hp Gnome. The remainder were two-seat trainers, named the 'two seat short body', 'long body' and 'side-by-side', which were powered by a 50hp, 70hp or 75hp Gnome.

General configuration of all the monoplanes was a wooden, wire-braced fuselage covered in fabric and parallel-chord wings, which used wing warping for lateral control. The tailplane was all-moving and was triangular or fan-shaped and, like the fin, was all-moving.

## Service
The first aircraft, P-1 No. 46, was intended to take part in the Gordon Bennett Cup race at Eastchurch on 1 July 1911 but was not ready in time. The next two P-1s built, No. 56 and No. 57, were for the Daily Mail Circuit of Britain race. However, No. 56, flown by Prier, crashed on the morning of the race and Oscar Morison, who was to fly No. 57, had been injured in an earlier incident and could not fly.

In October, Prier and James Valentine flew the two-seater, the No. 58, convincing the directors of Bristol that the aircraft was ready for bulk production and potential sales overseas. It made quite an impression at the Paris Salon de l' Aeronautique in December, no doubt helped by the fact that it was the only representative from Britain.

Demonstration flights across Europe followed including those carried out by Howard Pixton in Spain and Germany; the latter became the home of a German subsidiary named the Deutsche Bristolwerke Flugzeuggesellschaft, which also had its own flying school at Halberstadt.

The majority of Prier monoplanes were sold to civilians for training and racing but some military sales did take place including in Britain when the RFC took delivery of a pair of two-seaters. Aircraft were also sold to Italy, Turkey and Bulgaria for military use.

## Production

Three P-1s (Nos. 46, 56 and 57); seven single-school (Nos. 68, 81, 95–98 and 102); 11 two-seat short body (Nos. 58, 71–76, 83, 84, 90 and 94); ten two-seat long body (Nos. 82, 85–89, 91, 130, 155 and 156) and three two-seat side-by-side (Nos. 107–109), all built between July 1911 and December 1912.

| Technical data – Bristol-Prier P-1 | |
|---|---|
| ENGINE | One 50hp Gnome |
| WINGSPAN | 30ft 2in |
| LENGTH | 24ft 6in |
| WING AREA | 166sq ft |
| EMPTY WEIGHT | 640lb |
| ALL-UP WEIGHT | 820lb |
| SPEED | 68mph |

A trio of P-1 Bristol-Prier Monoplanes at Larkhill in August 1911, with No. 56 on the left, the first aircraft No. 46 in the centre and No. 57 on the right.

# Gordon England Biplanes

## Development
Eric Gordon England joined Bristol as a company staff pilot after gaining his Royal Aero Club aviator's certificate on 25 August 1911. England immediately expressed an interest in aircraft design and not long after arriving at the company, set to work on three machines called the Bristol-Gordon England Biplanes, GE.1, 2 and 3.

## Design
There was nothing particularly ground-breaking about the Gordon England (GE) Biplanes; they were conventional aircraft made of wood and fabric, braced by wooden struts and wire. The undercarriage was a traditional tail skid arrangement, while the main unit comprised a pair of wheels mounted on a central skid to help stop the machine tipping over on landing.

The first aircraft, the G.E.1, No. 64 was powered by a 50hp Clerget, while the two G.E.2s, were powered by a 70hp Daimler (No. 104) and a 100hp Gnome (No. 103). The G.E.2 was an improved military variant with modified wings, which were raised to give greater clearance for the propeller while on the ground. The G.E.3 made use of the wings of the G.E.2 and a completely redesigned cylindrical fuselage with power provided by an 80hp Gnome. The two crew were seated in tandem and the gap between each cockpit housed large brass fuel and oil tanks, the former being big enough to keep the G.E.3 flying for a good three hours. One main feature of these Gordon England machines was that the wings could be detached quickly and easily for transportation by road.

## Service
The sole G.E.1 first flew in May 1912, but the Clerget engine was underpowered and directional stability was poor, although the latter issue was solved by a larger balanced rudder. The G.E.1 was sold to the Deutsche Bristolwerke Flugzeuggesellschaft on 19 June 1912 but proved to be unsuitable for flying training and was returned to Bristol on 21 September and scrapped at Filton not long after.

The G.E.2s were entered into the Military Aeroplane Competition in August 1912, where they were demonstrated by Gordon England and Howard Pixton. The Daimler engine in No. 104 (competition No. 13) failed to deliver its maximum power forcing the aircraft to retire while the second G.E.2 was damaged in an accident and also had to be withdrawn.

The two G.E.3s were built to a Turkish government specification. The aircraft flew well enough but too much flex in the rear main spars, combined with an escalation of the Turkish-Italian war, resulted in no delivery being made and the project being abandoned.

## Production
In total, one G.E.1 (No. 64) two G.E.2s (Nos. 103 and 104) and two G.E.3s (Nos.112 and 113) were built.

| Technical data – Gordon England G.E.1, 2 and 3 | |
|---|---|
| ENGINE | (G.E.1) One 50hp Clerget; (G.E.2 No. 104) one 70hp Daimler; (G.E.2 No. 103) one 100hp Gnome; (G.E.3) one 80hp Gnome |
| WINGSPAN | (G.E.1) 33ft 8in; (G.E.2) 40ft; (G.E.3) 39ft |
| WING AREA | (G.E.1) 320sq ft; (G.E.2) 400sq ft; (G.E.3) 387sq ft |
| EMPTY WEIGHT | (G.E.2 No. 104) 1,100lb; (G.E.2 No. 103) 1,080lb; (G.E.3) 1,096lb |
| ALL-UP WEIGHT | (G.E.2 No. 104) 2,000lb; (G.E.2 No. 103) 1,980lb; (G.E.3) 1,996lb |
| SPEED | (G.E.1 and G.E.3) 65mph; (G.E.2 No. 104) 62mph; (G.E.2 No. 103) 68mph |

The second of only two Bristol-Gordon England G.E.3s to be built was No. 113, pictured at Filton in November 1912.

# Bristol-Coanda Monoplanes

## Development
A trained engineer and talented artist, Romanian-born Henri Coanda joined Bristol in January 1912. Coanda's first aircraft was displayed at the Paris Salon in 1910 and, like the monoplanes that he would design for Bristol, all his machines demonstrated features that would become commonplace.

## Design
Coanda's first aircraft was a two-seat in tandem mid-wing aircraft powered by 50hp Gnome, named the School Monoplane. Relatively orthodox in appearance, the design was developed into a similar training machine that had a side-by-side cockpit arrangement with dual controls; it was simply named the Side by Side Monoplane. Both aircraft were a development of the Prier Monoplane, with lateral control achieved by wing warping.

A pair of Competition Monoplanes powered by an 80hp Gnome gave Coanda the opportunity to design a very sleek-looking aircraft. This machine was developed into the Military Monoplane, which turned out to be the main production variant of the Coanda Monoplanes. Production aircraft were fitted with longer wingspans, had a greater fuel capacity and a bigger rudder. A single 70hp Daimler-powered Monoplane was also built but proved too heavy.

## Service
The School Monoplane was first trialled at Larkhill during March and April 1912 and, along with the Side-by-Side Monoplane, served with flying schools at Larkhill and Brooklands. A single School and a pair of Side-by-Sides were sold to Italy; and four Schools and three Side-by-Sides were sold to Coanda's native Romania. Another 36 Italian Military Monoplanes were to be built by Caproni and Faccanoni under licence but, following military aircraft trials in 1913, the licence was cancelled after only two aircraft were built. These aircraft, along with two Romanian machines and a pair sold to the Deutsche Bristolwerke Flugzeuggesellschaft, were returned to Filton in late 1913 and converted into T.B.8 biplanes.

The two Competition Monoplanes were purchased by the War Office to serve with the fledgling RFC after competing in the Military Aeroplane Competition in August 1912. Serialled 262 (No. 106) and 263 (No. 105), the latter was lost near Wolvercote, Oxford, on 10 September 1912, killing both officers on board.

## Production
Six School (Nos.77, 132, 185, 186, 188 and 189); seven Side by Side (Nos. 80, 110, 164–166, 176 and 177); two Competition (Nos. 105 and 106); one Daimler (No. 111) and 20 Military (Nos. 118, 121–123, 131, 142–154 and 196), one extra Military was supplied to Italy. A production licence was purchased by Caproni and Faccanoni at Varese but only two were built.

| Technical data – Bristol-Coanda Monoplanes | |
|---|---|
| ENGINE | (School and Side by Side) One 50hp Gnome; (Competition and Military) one 80hp Gnome; (Daimler) one 70hp Daimler |
| WINGSPAN | (School and Competition) 40ft; (Side by Side) 41ft 3in; (Daimler) 39ft 4in; (Military) 42ft 9in |
| LENGTH | (School and Side by Side) 27ft; (Competition) 28ft 3in; (Daimler) 30ft 9in; (Military) 29ft 2in |
| WING AREA | (School and Side by Side) 275sq ft; (Competition) 242sq ft; (Daimler) 260sq ft; (Military) 280sq ft |
| EMPTY WEIGHT | (School and Side by Side) 770lb; (Competition) 1,000lb; (Daimler) 1,200lb; (Military) 1,050lb |
| ALL-UP WEIGHT | (School and Side by Side) 1,100lb; (Competition) 1,710lb; (Daimler) 1,850lb; (Military) 1,775lb |
| SPEED | (School and Side by Side) 65mph; (Competition) 73mph; (Daimler) 60mph; (Military) 71mph |

Bristol Coanda Competition Monoplane No. 106 displaying its War Office Aeroplane Competition No. 14 in August 1912. Flown by test-pilot Harry Busteed during the competition, the aircraft finished joint third to win a prize of £500.

# Bristol-Burney Flying Boats

## Development
Experiments with Bristol-built aircraft that were capable of operating from water were first carried out by Howard Pixton in October 1911, using a Boxkite fitted with flotation bags under the wings. The flight, carried out from Hayling Island, had Lt Charles Dennistoun Burney, Royal Navy, on board, who was an enthusiastic supporter of the potential of Naval aircraft. Burney had a number of technical ideas for operating aircraft from water but lacked the resources needed to turn them into practical projects. After approaching Bristol with the support of the Admiralty, a new secret 'X Department' was created in late 1911 with Frank Barnwell as designer, assisted by Clifford Tinson.

## Design
The first of three designs was based on the G.E.1 biplane, which was modified with a 'water' undercarriage consisting of three 'hydropeds' each fitted with several hydrofoil vanes. While stationary, the aircraft would be supported in the water by five torpedo-shaped pneumatic floats under the wings and fuselage. Designated as the X.1, Barnwell proposed an inflatable wing for the aircraft, which would be covered in rubberised fabric. Ultimately it proved to be too heavy and the idea of the X.1 was abandoned.

The second design, the X.2 (No. 92), was approved for construction. The aircraft featured a fuselage planked like the hull of a boat, covered in thin mahogany veneer and finished with sailcloth and varnished. The wings were made up of three spars with warp control and covered in a waterproof varnish. Power was provided by an 80hp Canton-Unné water-cooled radial engine, which drove a traditional conventional two-blade propeller and a pair of water propellers positioned behind the two forward hydropeds.

The final design was the X.3 (No. 159), a larger aircraft than the X.2, which featured a fuselage covered in Consuta plywood. The positions of the water propellers were changed to a central location and were contra-rotating to remove the effects of torque. Ailerons replaced wing warping and more power was on hand in the shape of a 200hp Canton-Unné, which was loaned from the Admiralty.

## Service
The X.2 was loaded onto a lighter on 9 May 1912 and in secrecy was towed to Dale, Milford Have, where floatation trials were carried out. After a few leaks were plugged, taxying trials began, which revealed the aircraft moved off quickly using the water screws but the streamlined fairings around the hydroped tubes were ripped off by the friction of the water. Stability problems both above and below the water continued to plague the X.2 but while these were being rectified, it was decided to flight test the aircraft by towing it without the engine, which was replaced by 500lb of ballast. On 21 September 1912, with the controls locked for level flight, the X.2 was towed behind a torpedo boat. In a 12kt wind, the aircraft rose into the air at a mere 30kts with George Dacre on board, monitoring instruments. Before the aircraft had chance to gain a level path, the towing line was slipped and the X.2 stalled and crashed without injury to Dacre.

The X.3 performed preliminary taxying trials but, before flight testing could begin, the aircraft was grounded on a sandbank in June 1914 with Harry Busteed at the controls. The entire exercise did not go to waste from Lt Durney's point of view; the information gained would help in developing the Paravane.

| Technical data – Bristol-Burney X1, X2 and X3 | |
|---|---|
| **ENGINE** | (X1) One 60hp E.N.V; (X2) one 80hp Canton-Unné; (X3) one 200hp Canton-Unné |
| **WINGSPAN** | (X1) 34ft; (X2) 55ft 9in; (X3) 57ft 10in |
| **LENGTH** | (X1) 30ft; (X2) 30ft 8in; (X3) 36ft 8in |
| **WING AREA** | (X1) 325sq ft; (X2) 480sq ft; (X3) 500sq ft |

Harry Busteed taxies the Bristol-Burney X.3 during trials at Milford Haven in June 1914. Only moments later, the aircraft ran aground on a hidden sandbank causing serious damage. After approaching the Admiralty for more backing, which was refused, the project was closed down in July 1914.

# Bristol-Coanda Two-Seat Biplanes

## Development
From September 1912, the Military Wing RFC banned the flying of all monoplanes, immediately removing any potential for large military order for the Coanda monoplane. In the meantime, the B.E.2 biplane was entering production with a variety of manufacturers including Bristol, which prompted Coanda to design a biplane of his own. Within weeks, interest in this long-range, two-seat biplane was expressed by Germany and Spain.

## Design
The first Coanda Two-Seat Biplane was designated the B.R.7. This aircraft could accommodate the 80hp Gnome (as requested by Spain) and the 90hp Daimler-Mercedes (requested by Germany). Initially fitted with standard normal section monoplane wings, the B.R.7 flew much better once a set with a cambered profile was fitted, but a significant order did not materialise and only seven were built.

Coanda designed a central-float seaplane in January 1913 referred to as the No. 120 or 'Hydro'. Very similar in design to the G.E.3, the aircraft's main float was designed by Oscar Gnosspelius (it was later split in half and used for the T.B.8H 'Hydro' seaplane), which was replaced by SE Saunders of Cowes' much lighter float. It was powered by a closely cowled 80hp Gnome, which proved to be its undoing because the engine quickly overheated and was wrecked in September 1913 after power was lost.

The most successful of all the Coanda biplanes was the T.B.8 landplane, derived from the original monoplane. The aircraft featured two-bay wings, initially using wing warping for lateral control although later aircraft were fitted with ailerons. The T.B.8's slim fuselage could be fitted with a variety of engines and the undercarriage carried four wheels – larger to the rear while smaller ones were mounted forward in front of the propeller.

## Service
The only aircraft of this group to have reasonably successful service was the T.B.8 purchased for the RNAS and RFC. Three T.B.8s delivered to the RNAS at Gosport and Eastchurch in October 1914 were despatched to France. One of these aircraft bombed the German batteries at Middelkerke, Belgium, on 25 November 1914 and at least one aircraft was still in the service of 1 Squadron, RNAS, in February 1915 when it moved to France. Four 1 Squadron T.B.8s detached from Gosport would carry out coastal patrol duties from Newcastle-on-Tyne through the winter of 1914–15 and were the last operational machines. However, the type was still being ordered by the Admiralty in August 1915 to be used for training. A handful remained in this role until early 1917.

The T.B.8 also served with the Romanian Air Force, which had six Coanda monoplanes converted.

## Production
The following aircraft were built: one Hydro (No. 120), seven BR.7s (Nos. 157, 158, 160–163 and 178), one Daimler (constructed in Germany), 53 T.B.8s (Nos. 118, 121, 143, 144, 147–149, 151–153, 196–198, 218, 225, 227, 228, 331–342 and 870–893), one TB.8H (No. 205), one G.B.75 (No. 223) and one P.B.8 (No. 199).

| Technical data – Bristol-Coanda Hydro 120, B.R.7, G.B.75 and T.B.8 | |
|---|---|
| ENGINE | (120) One 80hp Gnome; (B.R.7) one 70hp Renault; (T.B.8) one 80hp, 80hp Le Rhône, 100hp Mono-Gnome, 50hp Gnome or 60 Le Rhône and (G.B.75) one 75hp Mono-Gnome |
| WINGSPAN | (120) 38ft 8in; (B.R.7) 38ft and (G.B.75 and T.B.8) 37ft 8in |
| LENGTH | (120) 27ft 10; (B.R.7) 27ft 5in and (T.B.8) 29ft 3in |
| WING AREA | (120) 436sq ft; (B.R.7) 440sq ft; (T.B.8) 450sq ft and (G.B.75) 420sq ft |
| EMPTY WEIGHT | (B.R.7) 946lb and (T.B.8 and G.B.75) 970lb |
| ALL-UP WEIGHT | (B.R.7) 1,826lb; (T.B.8) 1,665lb and (G.B.75) 1,650lb |
| SPEED | (B.R.7) 63mph; (T.B.8) 65 to 75mph and (G.B.75) 80mph |
| DURATION | 5hrs |

*Right*: The first Bristol-Coanda B.R.7, No. 157, being flown by Harry Busteed at Larkhill in 1913.

*Below*: The Romanian Prince Cantacuzène was so impressed with the performance of his T.B.8 conversions that he ordered an improved variant powered by a 75hp Monosoupape Gnome engine, designated the G.B.75. First flown at Larkhill on 7 April 1914, the order was cancelled in June.

# Scout Types A to D and S.S.A and S.2A

## Development
The successful story of the Bristol Scout began in November 1913, following failure of the Caproni-Bristol contract to build Coanda military monoplanes. Part of this contract was to supply a Coanda design called the S.B.5, but only the fuselage was completed and this was awaiting disposal. The fuselage caught the eye of Frank Barnwell who quickly adapted it to become the Scout A biplane.

## Design
The incomplete fuselage of the S.B.5 was finished and fitted with a set of 22ft-span single-bay wings plus redesigned tail surfaces. Also nicknamed the 'Baby Biplane', the first Scout was powered by an 80hp Gnome and, after trials, was fitted with increased-span wings, to improve the aircraft's slow speed performance. A pair of Scout Bs followed, almost identical to the A, other than underwing skids and a wider rudder.

The first main production variant was the Scout C (aka the Type 1), the first 36 of which featured dome-fronted cowls and a repositioned main oil tank behind the pilot. The latter resulted in a raised dorsal decking behind the cockpit to make room for the tank. Later production aircraft had an improved engine cowl and the oil tank was moved forward of the pilot.

The most prolific variant of all was the Scout D (aka the Type 2 to 5) with revised fuel and oil tanks. Later aircraft featured new increased dihedral wings and shorter ailerons. Armament for all Scouts was rudimentary at first but eventually settled to a single 0.303in Lewis machine-gun. In March 1916, Scout D became the first RFC aircraft to be fitted with synchronisation gear.

The final members of the Scout family were the Coanda-designed S.S.A featuring a bulletproof sheet-steel 'bath' to protect the pilot, petrol and oil tanks, and engine. The S.2A was a two-seat derivative of the Scout D.

## Service
The sole Scout A was trialled at Larkhill in February 1914 and later sold to Lord Carberry, who ditched the machine in the Channel during the London–Paris–London Air Race in July. The two Scout Bs, serialled 633 and 648, joined 3 and 5 Squadrons, RFC, in France and were furnished with various weapons. The Scout C saw widespread service with both RFC and RNAS squadrons, both of whom demanded priority when placing ever-growing orders with Bristol. The aircraft achieved early fame when Captain Lanoe G Hawker of 6 Squadron forced down three enemy aircraft armed only with a single-shot Martini carbine mounted at an angle on the starboard side of his aircraft; for his action he won the first Victoria Cross (VC) of aerial combat.

The Scout D, introduced in November 1915, also saw widespread service in the RFC, RNAS and Australian Flying Corps (AFC) and remained in production until late 1916.

## Production
One Scout A (No. 206), two Scout Bs (Nos. 229 and 230), 161 Scout Cs, 210 Scout Ds, one S.S.A (No. 219) and two S.2As (Nos. 1377 and 1378) were built.

| Technical data – Scout A–D, S.S.A. and S.2A | |
|---|---|
| ENGINE | (A) One 80hp Gnome or Le Rhône; (B) one 80hp Gnome Lambda; (C) one 80hp Gnome, Le Rhône or Clerget; (D) 80hp Gnome, Le Rhône or Clerget, 100hp Mono-Gnome, 110hp Clerget or Le Rhône; (S.S.A.) one 80hp Clerget or Gnome; (S.2A) one 110hp Clerget or 100hp Mono-Gnome |
| WINGSPAN | (A) 22ft and 24ft 7in; (B–D) 24ft 7in; (S.S.A.) 27ft 4in; (S.2A) 28ft 2in |
| LENGTH | (A) 19ft 9in; (B–D) 20ft 8in; (S.S.A.) 19ft 9in; (S.2A) 21ft 3in |
| WING AREA | (A) 161 and 198sq ft; (B–D) 198sq ft; (S.S.A.) 200sq ft |
| EMPTY WEIGHT | (A) 617lb and 750lb; (B) 750lb; (C) 760lb; (D) 760lb and 925lb; (S.S.A) 913lb |
| ALL-UP WEIGHT | (A) 957lb and 1,100lb; (B) 1,100lb; (C and S.S.A) 1,200lb; (D) 1,250lb and 1,440lb; (S.2A) 1,400lb |
| MAX SPEED | (A) 95 and 100mph; (B) 100mph; (C) 93mph; (D) 100 and 110mph; (S.S.A.) 106mph; (S.2A) 95mph |
| RATE OF CLIMB | (A) 800 ft/min; (B and C) 1,000 ft/min; (D) 1,100 ft/min |

*Right*: One of several Scout Ds to be converted with a 110hp Clerget engine, a semi-spherical spinner and much larger ailerons.

*Below*: The one and only Scout A, No. 206, during preliminary flight trials at Larkhill in February 1914. The Scout was nicknamed 'Baby Biplane' because of its diminutive size.

# T.T.A and F.3A

## Development
In September 1915, Frank Barnwell, who had joined Bristol the previous month, produced a design for a twin-engined local defence fighter in collaboration with Leslie G Frise.

## Design
The design of this new aircraft was to a War Office requirement with the promise of four RAF 4a engines being supplied to power a pair of prototype aircraft. Designated the T.T.A. (T.T. stands for Twin Tractor), the aircraft was a two-seat, twin-engine aircraft, which endeavoured to be and provide a good field of fire for the gunner. The latter was positioned forward, while the pilot was located behind the trailing edge of the wing; both were given a 0.303in Lewis machine gun. Following large demand for the RAF 4a for the BE.12 and RE.8, Bristol was allocated four 120hp Beadmores instead. Two prototypes were ordered on 15 February 1916 at a unit price minus the engine cost of £2,000.

While the T.T.A. was under construction, a number of 250hp Rolls-Royce engines became available and Bristol was invited to tender for an anti-Zeppelin fighter. Bristol's design was designated the F.3A, a three-seat single-engined aircraft of which two prototypes were ordered on 16 May 1916. The F.3A made use of the T.T.A.'s wings, rear fuselage and tail unit but was cancelled before an aircraft had been completed.

## Service
Allocated the RFC serials 7750 and 7751, the former made its maiden flight in the hands of Capt Hooper, the CO of RFC Acceptance Park, Filton, on 26 April 1916, followed by the latter on 27 May. The 7750 was flown to Upavon, Wiltshire, on 11 May for acceptance trials and recorded a maximum speed of 87mph and an initial climb rate of 400ft per minute. Despite the promising performance figures, the T.T.A. was an unpopular aircraft not recommended for squadron service.

## Production
In total, two T.T.As were built (Nos. 1375 and 1376) and given RFC serials 775 and 7751. Two F.3As were ordered (to be serial No. 1485 and 1486) on 16 May 1916 and were allocated RFC serials A612 and A613, but were cancelled.

| Technical data – T.T.A and F.3A | |
|---|---|
| ENGINE | (T.T.A) Two 120hp Beardmore; (F.3A) one 250hp Rolls-Royce |
| WINGSPAN | 53ft 6in |
| LENGTH | (T.T.A) 39ft 2in; (F.3A) 36ft 5in |
| WING AREA | 817sq ft |
| EMPTY WEIGHT | (T.T.A) 3,820lb and (F.3A) 3,400lb |
| ALL-UP WEIGHT | (T.T.A) 5,100lb; (F.3A) 5,300lb |
| CLIMB RATE | (T.T.A) 400 ft/min |
| MAX SPEED | (T.T.A) 87mph |

The second Bristol T.T.A. No. 7751, at Filton in May 1916.

# M.1A, M.1B and M.1C Monoplane Scouts

## Development
Designed in response to the successes achieved by the Fokker E type monoplanes against the RFC's poorly armed biplanes, the Bristol M.1 Monoplane Scout was a Frank Barnwell design that was ahead of its time and seemingly completely unappreciated during World War One.

## Design
Incorporating all the experience gleaned from the Scout D, Frank Barnwell's next design was an aerodynamically clean aircraft. It was designed around a closely cowled radial engine, the diameter of which dictated the size of the fuselage to make the machine as streamlined as possible. The fuselage was conventional, made up of four longeron girders internally wire braced. The monoplane wings were attached to the upper longerons and wire braced to the lower longeron and above to a substantial cabane strut, which doubled to protect the pilot in the event of the aircraft turning over. The undercarriage was a basic V-type mounted with a pair of wheels attached to a rubber-sprung cross-axle.

The sole M.1A was a private venture, which resulted in an order for four M.1Bs that were fitted with a single Vickers machine gun mounted on the port side of the forward fuselage, a cut-out panel in the starboard wing root and a revised cabane strut. The main production version, the M.1C, featured a 110hp Le Rhône, a Vickers machine gun mounted in front of the pilot, cut-outs in both wing-roots to improve downward visibility and many more operational refinements.

## Service
The first in the series, the M.1A, carried out its maiden flight on 14 July 1916 in the hands of F.P. Raynham. During trials at the Central Flying School (CFS), the aircraft performed well and a tentative order for another M.1A and four M.1Bs was placed. The latter delivered from December 1916, were powered by various engines and were trialled at the CFS also by 50 (March 1917) and 111 Squadrons. A landing speed of 49mph was deemed too high for them to operate from the small French airfields of the Western Front. A more substantial order for 125 aircraft was made in August 1917 for a main production variant designated as the M.1C. Virtually all were relegated to units operating in the Middle East, including 47 (February to May 1918), 63 (January to December 1919), 72 (March 1918 to February 1919) and 150 (April 1918 to February 1919) squadrons.

## Production
One M.1A (A5138), four M.1Bs (A5139–A5142) and 125 M.1Cs (C4901–C5025) were produced; the latter production order was issued on 3 August 1917 and delivered between 19 September 1917 and 25 February 1918.

| Technical data – M.1A, M.1B and M.1C Monoplane Scouts | |
|---|---|
| ENGINE | (A and B) One 110hp Le Clerget; (C) one 110hp Le Rhone; (B) one 130hp Clerget or 150hp A.R.1 |
| WINGSPAN | 30ft 9in |
| LENGTH | 20ft 4in |
| WING AREA | 145sq ft |
| EMPTY WEIGHT | 900lb |
| ALL-UP WEIGHT | 1,350lb |
| MAX SPEED | (A) 132mph; (B) 125mph; (C) 130mph |
| SERVICE CEILING | (A) 17,000ft; (B) 15,000ft; (C) 20,000ft |
| ENDURANCE | (A) 2¾hrs; (C) 1¾hrs |

**Around 130 M.1 Monoplane Scouts were built, all by the Bristol & Colonial Aeroplane Co. Ltd. There were two M.1As, four M.1Bs, 125 M.1Cs and a single M.1D; the latter being a conversion of an M.1B rebuilt in 1922 with a 100hp Bristol Lucifer radial engine.**

# F.2A and F.2B Fighter

## Development
Bristol's chief designer, Frank Barnwell, added the final touches to the design of a two-seat reconnaissance aircraft, which in competition with the RAF RE.8, would be the long overdue replacement for the B.E.2 in March 1916.

## Design
Initially designed as the R.2A (Type 9) with a 120hp Beardmore engine and again as the R.2B (Type 9A) with a 150hp Hispano-Suiza, the F.2A (Type 12) would be the first prototype when the excellent 190hp Rolls-Royce Falcon I became available. Designed as a two-seat reconnaissance machine, the compact F.2A was armed with a single, synchronised forward-firing 0.303in Vickers and a single 0.303in Lewis mounted on a Scarff ring in the rear observer's cockpit. The main production version, the F.2B (Type 14) featured modifications including a larger fuel tank and bigger ammunition boxes. Early production F.2Bs were powered by the Falcon I although the bulk were fitted with the 275hp Falcon III.

The F.2C (Type 22) was used for testing an experimental range of engines while the F.2B Mk II, first flown in December 1919, was built for army co-operation duties in tropical climates. A structurally strengthened version, the Fighter Mk III (Type 96) was also produced as late as 1926. The Fighter Mk IV (Type 96A) was a conversion of the Mk III airframe with further improved strength.

## Service
The prototype F.2A, A3303, first flew from Filton on 9 September 1916. The type entered service in February 1917 with 48 Squadron. It had an inauspicious entry into combat when, in April 1917, a patrol of six aircraft was reduced to two when it encountered Richthofen's Jasta 11. The losses were no fault of the aircraft but were due to the poor tactics employed and, with the introduction of the definitive F.2B Fighter, it was realised that 'Brisfit' as it was also known, could be thrown around like many of its contemporary fighters. With a higher-powered Falcon engine than the F.2A, the F.2B was more than 10mph faster with a maximum speed of 123mph and could reach 10,000ft three minutes faster than its predecessor. Making full use of the fixed-forward firing machine-gun instead of relying upon the gunner in the rear cockpit made the 'Brisfit' a tough opponent to any German fighter right up to the end of World War One.

The F.2B remained in RAF service until 1932 and also saw service in Australia, Belgium, Canada, Ireland, Greece, Mexico, New Zealand, Norway, Peru and Spain. A total of 5,329 'Brisfits' were built at Filton including by a host of sub-contractors.

## Production
Total production of the F.2 Fighter family was 5,308 aircraft, built by Bristol at Filton and Brislington. Sub-contractors were Angus Sanderson, Armstrong Whitworth, Austin Motors, Cunard Steamship, Gloucestershire, Harris and Sheldon, Standard Motors in Britain and Curtiss, Dayton-Wright and Engineering Division – Bureau of Aircraft Production in the USA.

## Technical data – F.2A and F.2B Fighter

| | |
|---|---|
| ENGINE | (A) One 190hp Rolls-Royce Falcon I, 220hp Falcon II, 275hp Falcon III or 150hp or 200hp Hispano-Suiza; (B) one 200 Sunbeam Arab, 200hp RAF 4d, 180hp Wolseley Viper, 230 Siddeley Puma or 300hp Hispano-Suiza |
| WINGSPAN | 39ft 3in |
| LENGTH | (Falcon) 25ft 10in; (Arab & Hispano) 24ft 10in; (Puma) 26ft |
| HEIGHT | 9ft 6in |
| WING AREA | (A) 389sq ft; (B) 405sq ft |
| EMPTY WEIGHT | (A-Falcon I) 1,700lb; (B-Falcon III) 2,095lb |
| ALL-UP WEIGHT | (A-Falcon I) 2,700lb; (B-Falcon III) 3,160lb |
| MAX SPEED | (A-Falcon I) 110mph; (B-Falcon III) 115mph |
| SERVICE CEILING | 20,000ft |
| ENDURANCE | 3hrs |

*Right*: For many years, the Shuttleworth Collection's F.2B Fighter, D8096, was the world's only airworthy example. This popular aircraft has now been joined by D7889 in Canada and D8084 in New Zealand.

*Below*: A rare photograph shows an F.2A in service with 48 Squadron at La Bellevue, Northern France. The unit operated the F.2A from March until July 1917.

# M.R.1 Metal Biplane

## Development
As World War One progressed and aircraft production expanded rapidly across the country, stocks of timber, namely silver spruce, began to decline. Metal was the obvious alternative but early efforts to produce such machines had resulted in overweight flying machines that took a great deal of time to produce. Vickers and Junkers were already making good progress and Bristol had been penning ideas since 1914, but metal structures were pushed to the forefront as the supply of wood looked in doubt.

## Design
In 1916, Frank Barnwell submitted his design for two-seat reconnaissance aircraft, designated the M.R.1 (M.R. standing for Metal Reconnaissance) and won a contract for a pair of aircraft. With maritime experience behind him, Barnwell incorporated varnished duralumin sheets to combat corrosion. The fuselage was made up of a pair of semi-monocoque forward sections braced by upper longitudinal members to which an 140hp Hispano-Suiza water-cooled engine was mounted. Two more monocoque sections housed the pilot and observer and tail unit. The fuselage was rectangular in cross section although the corners were rounded. The wings, initially planned to be metal, were conventional in design and made of wood with ailerons attached to the upper mainplane only.

## Service
The first M.R.1, serialled A5177 (2067) was delivered to the Air Board on 23 October 1917 for £1,600, reduced from £2,000 because of the wooden wings. By 1918, metal wings were added to the A5177 and helped provide Bristol and the military with useful information.

The second machine, A5178 (2068), did not fly until 1918 and was fitted with an 180hp Wolseley Viper. After the end of World War One, the A5178 was regularly flown by Barnwell before being accepted by the RAE at Farnborough on 19 April 1919. However, Barnwell who was flying A5178, struck a pine tree near the north gate and crash landed on the airfield. He escaped serious injury but the M.R.1 was wrecked and subsequently not repaired.

## Production
Two aircraft were built by Bristol at Filton serialled A5177 and A5178 (No. 2067 and 2068); the wings were built by The Steel Wing Company of Gloucester.

| Technical data – M.R.1 Metal Biplane | |
| --- | --- |
| ENGINE | One 140hp Hispano-Suiza or 180hp Wolseley Viper |
| WINGSPAN | 42ft 2in |
| LENGTH | 27ft |
| HEIGHT | 10ft 3in |
| WING AREA | 458sq ft |
| EMPTY WEIGHT | 1,700lb |
| ALL-UP WEIGHT | 2,810lb |
| MAX SPEED | 110mph |
| ENDURANCE | 5hrs |

The Bristol M.R.1 A.58623 (originally serialled A5177) after metal wings had been fitted at Filton in 1918.

# Scout E and F

## Development
By late 1916, the power that could be gleaned from an air-cooled radial engine had reached its peak and both engine and aircraft designers turned to the water-cooled in-line engine. The Hispano-Suiza was about to enter service with the excellent SE.5a, but even this engine did not prove to be as reliable as hoped during early service. Wilfrid Reid produced preliminary drawings for a single-seat biplane to be powered by a proposed 200hp 'Cruciform' ten-cylinder radial but, when this engine failed to appear, the design was revised with a 200hp Hispano-Suiza and designated the Scout F.

## Design
Reid's initial design, called the Scout E, was revised by Frank Barnwell into a small biplane with unequal-span wings and ailerons, which were only fitted to the upper mainplane. A pair of synchronised 0.303in Vickers machine guns were mounted side-by-side in the upper forward fuselage. On the receipt of a contract to build six Scout Fs on 4 June 1917, the powerplant was changed to a Sunbeam Arab V-8 water-cooled engine because of a shortage of Hispano-Suizas, which were fitted instead into SE.5As.

While the fitment of the Arab posed no problems, a large number of finer modifications took time so the final design was not completed until November 1917. By then, the few Sunbeam Arabs that had been tested had already demonstrated problems with vibration so it was decided only to fit them into the first two aircraft, serialled B3989 and B3990. As a result, the third aircraft B3991, was fitted with a 315hp Cosmos Mercury and designated the Scout F.1.

## Service
The first Scout F, B3989 made its maiden flight in March 1918 and the aircraft immediately impressed with a top speed of 138mph at sea level and only 10mph less at 10,000ft. The second aircraft, B3990, was delivered to the CFS where it was flown by well-known fighter pilots who praised the Scout for its aerobatic performance. The Scout F.1, B3991, first flew from Filton in the hands of Uwins on 4 September 1918. This was the first of many Bristol prototypes to be flown by Uwins.

The end of World War One arrested any chance of a large production order but the Scout F.1 continued to perform well and was delivered to Farnborough in December 1918. In April 1919, D3991 achieved two 'unofficial' records when the fighter reached 10,000ft in 5 min 24 secs and 20,000ft in 16 min 15 secs.

## Production
Four Scout Fs were built with serial numbers B3989 to B3992 (No. 2845–2848), although the last aircraft was only completed as an airframe. Two more aircraft were still incomplete by April 1919 and were not issued with Bristol manufacturer's numbers.

| Technical data – Scout F | |
|---|---|
| ENGINE | One 200hp Sunbeam Arab or one 315hp Cosmos Mercury |
| WINGSPAN | 29ft 7in |
| LENGTH | (Arab) 20ft 10in; (Mercury) 20ft 8in |
| WING AREA | 260sq ft |
| EMPTY WEIGHT | 1,440lb |
| ALL-UP WEIGHT | (Arab) 2,200lb; (Mercury) 2,260lb |
| MAX SPEED | (Arab) 138mph; (Mercury) 145mph |
| RATE OF CLIMB | (Arab) 9½ minutes to 10,000ft; (Mercury) 5½ minutes to 10,000ft |

The purposeful-looking Scout F.1, B3991 was powered by the Fedden and Butler-designed 315hp Cosmos Mercury engine manufactured by Brazil Starker & Co. Ltd of Fishponds, Bristol.

# Braemar, Pullman and Tramp

## Development
By mid-1917, a succession of Gotha raids on Britain were taking their toll on the public's morale and, as a result, the Independent Air Force was formed in October to attack industrial targets in Germany. Large, long-range bombers would be needed and both Handley Page and Bristol submitted designs.

## Design
Designed in October 1917, the Barnwell-designed B.1 was a big triplane capable of carrying six 250lb bombs internally. The power arrangement was unique, with an engine room containing four powerplants that drove two large four-bladed propellers via geared shafts. Once the B.1 was passed on to Wilfrid Reid, a more conservative design, renamed Braemar (Type 24), was produced to a traditional layout of four engines mounted in tandem pairs, driving a pair of pusher propellers. The second Braemar II (Type 25) was fitted with more powerful Liberty engines, which improved the climb rate with a full load by some margin.

A third Braemar was completed as the Pullman (Type 26). It was designed to carry 14 passengers in high comfort while the crew flew the aircraft from an enclosed cabin; this was an unpopular feature at the time. The basic design of the Braemar was extended further with the Tramp (Type 37) powered by four Armstrong Siddeley Puma engines mounted in Barnwell's original 'engine room' idea. Complex transmission systems meant that neither aircraft flew. At the same time, an ambitious steam-powered flying boat, of similar proportions to a Porte-type hull, was set out by Major Vernon. As with all early steam systems, weight was the problem and the idea was shelved.

## Service
The Braemar I, C4296 was first flown by test-pilot Fred Raynham on 13 August 1918 with under-powered 230 Siddeley Puma engines, rather than the intended 360hp Rolls-Royce Eagles. Exactly one month later, Raynham delivered C4296 to Martlesham Heath where, despite being under-powered, it achieved some very creditable performance figures as well as criticism of many details. All of these were rectified in Braemar II, C4297 first flown by Cyril Uwins on 18 February 1919. By then, the need for a long-range heavy bomber had passed and in April 1919, the Air Board recommended that the intended third Braemar should be built as civil transport.

After creating a sensation at the International Aero Show at Olympia in May 1920, the Pullman was delivered to Martlesham Heath and purchased outright on 7 September. The luxurious Pullman never flew a single fare-paying passenger and was later broken up.

## Production
Total production included one Braemar I, C4296 (No. 3751), one Braemar II, C4297 (No. 3752), one Pullman, C4298/G-EASP (No. 3753), and two Tramps, J6912 and J6913 (Nos.5871 and 5872).

| Technical data – Braemar I, II, Pullman and Tramp | |
|---|---|
| ENGINE | (I and Tramp) Four 230hp Siddeley Puma; (II and Pullman) four 400hp Liberty 12 |
| WINGSPAN | (I, II and Pullman) 81ft 8in; (Tramp) 96ft |
| LENGTH | (I and II) 51ft 6in; (Pullman) 52ft; (Tramp) 60ft |
| HEIGHT | 20ft |
| WING AREA | (I, II and Pullman) 1,905sq ft; (Tramp) 2,284sq ft |
| EMPTY WEIGHT | (I and II) 10,650lb; (Pullman) 11,000lb; (Tramp) 12,809lb |
| ALL-UP WEIGHT | (I) 16,500lb; (II) 18,000lb; (Pullman) 17,750lb; (Tramp) 18,795lb |
| MAX SPEED | (I) 106mph; (II) 125mph; (Pullman) 135mph |
| CEILING | (I) 14,000ft; (II) 17,000ft; (Pullman) 15,000ft |
| ACCOMMODATION | (I and II) Four crew; (Pullman) two crew and 14 passengers; (Tramp) three crew |

The Braemar II, C4297, pictured at Martlesham Heath, Suffolk, not long after it was delivered by test-pilot Cyril Uwins on 17 April 1919. The bomber returned to Filton, and later was wrecked after colliding with a hangar on Martlesham Heath in November 1921.

# F.2C Badger I, II and X

## Development
The Bristol F.2C first appeared in February 1917, a Falcon-powered version of the successful F.2B but lay dormant until October of that year. That month, a requirement for a new two-seat reconnaissance aircraft was issued to be designed with rapid production in mind. Bristol turned back to F.2C, a designation that would ultimately be discarded in place of the name Badger.

## Design
A single-bay biplane with prominently staggered wings unswept and unequal, the Badger was designed for a crew of two accommodated in tandem. Frank Barnwell originally planned for a 260hp Salmson radial to power the Badger or a Bentley B.R.2, neither of which would be powerful enough. At least 300hp would be needed to get the 3,000lb aircraft into the air and the first design was submitted for a 320hp Dragonfly in the Badger I. The Mk II would be powered by a 400hp Cosmos Jupiter I, while the civilian Badger X only needed a 230hp Puma engine; the latter of which was not built to a military specification.

## Service
Awarded an experimental contract to build three Badger Mk Is, the first aircraft, F3495, made its maiden flight on 4 February 1919. Unfortunately, the aircraft suffered an airlock on take-off and with a lifeless engine, Uwins was forced to crash land, ripping off the undercarriage and destroying the engine mounting. Quickly repaired and given a modified cowling and larger rudder, F3495 was delivered to the Air Board on 15 February.

The second Badger Mk I, F3496, ordered with a Jupiter engine, first flew on 24 May with a Dragonfly instead and was bought by the Air Board in September 1919. Not satisfied with the two aircraft that they had already received, the order for the third Badge Mk I was cancelled. A single Badger Mk II, J6492, was also ordered by the Air Board, powered by the 400hp Cosmos Jupiter. It was purchased by the Air Council in March 1920 and used for developmental testing of the Jupiter engine.

The Badger Mk X, which was built at a cost of just £250, was the first Bristol aircraft to enter onto the British Civil Register as K110, revised to G-EABU on 30 May 1919. After making its maiden flight on 13 May 1919, the aircraft was damaged beyond economic repair by Frank Barnwell just nine days later.

## Production
Three Badger Mk Is, F3495 to F3497 (Nos. 4254–4256), one Badger Mk II, J6492 (No. 5657) and one Badger Mk X serialled K110, later G-EABU (No. 5658), were built.

| Technical data – Badger I, II and X | |
|---|---|
| ENGINE | (I) One 320hp A.B.C. Dragonfly Ia; (II) one 400hp Cosmos Jupiter I; (X) 230hp Siddeley Puma |
| WINGSPAN | (I and II) 36ft 9in; (X) 34ft 2in |
| LENGTH | (I and II) 23ft 8in; (X) 24ft |
| HEIGHT | (I and II) 9ft 1in; (X) 9ft |
| WING AREA | (I and II) 357sq ft; (X) 340sq ft |
| EMPTY WEIGHT | (I and II) 1,950lb |
| ALL-UP WEIGHT | (I and II) 3,150lb |
| MAX SPEED | (I) 135mph; (II) 142mph |
| CEILING | (I) 19,000ft; (II) 20,600ft |

First flown by Uwins on 24 May 1919, the second Badger Mk I, F3496 is fitted with a 400hp Cosmos Jupiter I nine-cylinder radial engine. This was later developed into the Bristol Jupiter.

# Tourer and Coupé

## Development
As the end of World War One approached, thoughts began to turn towards the civilian market, and Frank Barnwell was given the opportunity to look at aircraft with the potential to carry two or three passengers. His first design was called the Rancher, but it never left the drawing board.

## Design
The Tourer's story began when Sir Frederick Sykes, the Controller of Civil Aviation, placed an order for three unarmed, Falcon-engined, two-seat communication aircraft. They were fitted with dual controls and their larger fuel tanks gave an endurance of up to five hours. A fourth aircraft, serialled H1460, was fitted with a hinged cover over the passenger seat and it was this machine that was retrospectively named the Bristol Coupé (Type 27) in 1920. The Tourer (Type 29) followed, and this aircraft was installed with the Puma engine from the Badger X; this aircraft was initially used as an engine test bed before becoming the first Tourer.

A two-seater version in side-by-side configuration was also built with the option of a coupé top. The open version was designated the Type 47, while the coupé was retrospectively designated the Type 28. A pair of three-seat Seaplanes (Type 48) had open cockpits, the first of which flew from Avonmouth, Bristol, on 15 October 1920.

Sub-variants of the Tourer family included the Scandinavian Tourer (Type 45) with the option of a ski undercarriage; the Puma Trainer (Type 81 and Type 81A); Greek Tourer (Type 86); and the Bulgarian Trainer (Type 88).

## Service
The Coupé made its first flights in May 1919 when civil aviation was allowed following the lifting of restrictions imposed during World War One. Interest began to gain momentum following the Paris Salon in December 1919, with the aircraft on display sold in the USA in May 1920, followed by the sale of a Type 28 and four Type 47s. The majority of the Tourers built were exported to customers in Australia, Newfoundland and Spain. Six Type 28 Tourers were bought by Major Norman Brearley for Western Australian Airways' weekly main service between Geraldton and Perth inaugurated on 4 December 1921.

Both the Puma Trainer and the Greek Tourer were sold to the Greek government. Four Trainers were used by the Filton Reserve Flying School, opened 15 May 1923.

## Production
Total production reached 33 aircraft, made up of one standard Coupé, 12 two-seaters, ten three-seaters, eight three-seater Type 47s, and two Seaplanes.

| Technical data – Tourer and Coupé, 2-seater, 3-seater Coupé, 3-seater Type 47s (Open) and Seaplane ||
|---|---|
| ENGINE | (Coupé) One 275hp Rolls-Royce Falcon III; (All others) one 230hp Siddeley Puma |
| WINGSPAN | (Coupé) 39ft 3in; (All others) 39ft 5in |
| LENGTH | (Coupé) 25ft 10in; (Seaplane) 29ft 6in; (All others) 26ft 1in |
| HEIGHT | (Coupé) 9ft 6in; (Seaplane) 11ft 5in; (All others) 10ft |
| WING AREA | (Coupé) 405sq ft; (All others) 407sq ft |
| EMPTY WEIGHT | (Coupé, three-seat Coupé and Open) 1,900lb; (two-seater) 1,700lb; (Seaplane) 2,100lb |
| ALL-UP WEIGHT | (Coupé and two-seater) 2,800lb; (All others) 3,000lb |
| MAX SPEED | (Coupé) 128mph; (two and three-seat Coupé) 120mph; (three-seat Open) 117mph; (Seaplane) 110mph |
| CEILING | (Coupé) 24,000ft; (two-seat) 22,000ft; (three-seat Coupé and Open) 20,000ft; (Seaplane) 17,000ft |

One of several Tourers sold in Britain was Type 47, G-EART, which was purchased by Instone Air Lines on 3 June 1920. Painted in the company's blue and white livery, the Tourer operated until February 1921.

# Babe

## Development
Not only was Frank Barnwell an excellent aircraft designer, he was also an enthusiastic pilot keen on cheap-to-operate and easy-to-fly machines for private owners. Originally named 'Barnwell's Bobby', the Babe was influenced by 30hp A.B.C. Gnat-powered Kittens, which Barnwell had observed during World War One.

## Design
A diminutive design, the Babe was originally planned for a 60hp A.B.C. Gadfly engine but, despite an order being placed, the company stopped building aero-engines and concentrated on motorbikes instead. In the meantime, Barnwell had remembered that he had worked with AV Roe back in 1911 on a small biplane powered by a 35hp Viale engine. The engine, which was damaged, had been in storage in Manchester ever since and, after a deal was struck, Barnwell brought the Viale back to Filton, where it was repaired and installed.

Unsurprisingly a single-seater, the Babe had a plywood-skinned fuselage that was fabric-covered for added protection. The wings were staggered and un-swept and full-span ailerons were only fitted to the upper mainplane. Barnwell redesigned the wings in 1920, producing a thick-section cantilever monoplane instead, which was installed to the first aircraft. The latter never flew.

## Service
The maiden flight of the first Babe Mk I took place sooner than expected because, on 28 November 1919, Uwins was forced into the air to avoid sheep having only planned to carry out taxiing trials! The aircraft was easy enough to fly in experienced hands but much trickier for the novice and the Viale engine proved to be too unreliable to sell on the open market.

An ultra-light 60hp Le Rhône rotary was fitted instead and the first two aircraft built were redesignated as the Babe Mk III. The second aircraft was registered as G-EAQD and with a Le Rhône made its maiden flight on 18 December 1919, followed by the re-engined first aircraft, G-EASQ on 14 April 1920.

A third aircraft, the Babe Mk II, powered by a Siddeley Ounce engine, never flew and was not registered. By late 1920, the civilian registrations had lapsed and presumably the aircraft were scrapped not long after. The original Viale engine, which belonged to Barnwell, remained in store until 1959 and after restoration, was donated to the Science Museum in London where it has been on display since 1963.

## Production
Three aircraft were built, manufacturer's numbers 5865, 5866 and 5875 (fitted with the Ounce engine). Only the first two were registered as G-EASQ and G-EAQD respectively. The third aircraft, designated the Babe Mk II, did not fly and was never registered.

| Technical data – Babe | |
|---|---|
| ENGINE | One 45hp Viale, one 40hp Siddeley Ounce or one 60hp Le Rhône |
| WINGSPAN | 19ft 8in |
| LENGTH | 14ft 11in |
| HEIGHT | 5ft 9in |
| WING AREA | 108sq ft |
| EMPTY WEIGHT | 460lb |
| ALL-UP WEIGHT | (Viale) 683lb; (Le Rhône) 840lb |
| MAX SPEED | (Viale) 85mph; (Le Rhône) 107mph |
| CEILING | (Viale) 10,000ft; (Le Rhône) 15,000ft |

The Babe Mk I in November 1919 with the original 35hp Viale five-cylinder radial. The engine was designed by the Italian engineer Spirito Mario Viale and built in France.

# Bullet

## Development
The Bristol Type 32 Bullet was an attempt to produce a flying demonstrator for the company's new Cosmos Jupiter radial engine. It was designed by Frank Barnwell and finalized in August 1919 and confidently predicted to be an outstanding performer; it would promote engine sales and receive prestige on behalf of the company by winning air races at home and abroad.

## Design
A single-seat biplane, the Bullet was built to be incredibly strong and every effort was made to keep the aircraft as aerodynamic as possible. The fuselage was conventional in its construction, its diameter being dictated by size of the 450hp Jupiter II engine, which would not be available until June 1920. Both wings and tailplane spars allowed for the use of very thin low-drag aerofoils and, in order to keep the landing speed below 50mph, a wing of 295sq ft was initially selected. The wings were of equal span, had ailerons fitted to the upper mainplane and the wing roots were joined to each other and the cabane struts along the upper centreline of the fuselage.

## Service
The Bullet (No. 5869) first appeared in public at the Paris Salon in December 1919 with a mock-up of a Cosmos Jupiter engine, made up of a dummy wooden crankcase with a plain airscrew. Once the engine was fitted, the aircraft was registered as G-EATS and the airworthy Bullet first appeared at the Aerial Derby on 24 July 1920. Cyril Uwins flew the Bullet to third place, achieving a disappointing average speed of just 129mph.

A new engine cowling was fitted and a hemispherical spinner, but when it was flown again, the anticipated improvement in performance failed to materialize. Further modifications included reducing the span of the wings (making a total wing area of 180sq ft), adding ailerons to the lower mainplane and giving a dihedral to the lower mainplane. The Bullet did not re-appear until February 1921, by which time flight testing of the Jupiter engine became a priority because it was now officially a Bristol product; a task that the Bullet carried out with the Badger.

The Bullet did enter the 1921 Aerial Derby, this time achieving an average speed of 141mph with Uwins at the controls again and finished fourth overall. Further tweaks followed but the most significant improvement was achieved by removing the large spinner. In this form, the Bullet was flown by Rollo de Haga Haig in the 1922 Aerial Derby where it recorded an average speed of 145mph and finished second. The cowling was improved again in January 1923 and during that year it was entered for the Aerial Derby and King's Cup Air Races with hopes of exceeding 175mph. However, following the death of Leslie Foot in that year, the Bullet was withdrawn, placed into storage then scrapped in 1924.

| Technical data – Bullet | |
|---|---|
| ENGINE | One 450hp Bristol Jupiter II |
| WINGSPAN | (early) 31ft 2in; (late) 22ft 4in |
| LENGTH | 24ft 1in |
| HEIGHT | (early) 9ft 8in; (late) 8ft 10in |
| WING AREA | (early) 295sq ft; (late) 180sq ft |
| EMPTY WEIGHT | 1,800lb |
| ALL-UP WEIGHT | 2,300lb |
| MAX SPEED | (early) 155mph; (late) 170mph |

Registered as G-EATS in June 1920, the sole Bullet rolled out at Filton the following month with original fairing and large span, 31ft 2in wings.

# Seely

## Development

To encourage aircraft designs with safety and comfort in mind, the Air Ministry announced the rules for a competition in July 1919. There were several different categories for both big and small aircraft and a wide range of points to be won for payload, economy, the ability to fly slowly and to take-off in a short distance.

## Design

To meet the rules, Bristol produced a derivative of the F.2B Coupé, the new aircraft, to be named the Seely. A two-seater aircraft, the pilot was positioned in an open cockpit while the sole passenger was accommodated in an enclosed cabin directly behind. The passenger's comfortable cabin had a raised roof and windows in the upper decking.

A great deal of thought had been given to safety in the event of a crash landing because the deep forward fuselage was made of steel tube rather than spruce, the former affording better protection. Multi-disc brakes were also fitted and a central skid to stop the aircraft from tipping over on landing. A three-bay biplane, the wing had a larger area than the Tourer, ailerons were fitted to both sets of mainplanes and a horn-balanced rudder and large fin were also fitted. Power was provided by a 240hp Puma cooled by a large radiator in the nose that proved to be very effective at low-climbing speeds.

## Service

It is not clear when the Seely first flew but the aircraft was registered as G-EAUE on 3 July 1920. The following month the competition began at Martlesham with the Seely in the same category as the

Westland Limousine and the Sopwith Antelope. Flown by Uwins, the Seely performed well in all tests although the Limousine, flown by Arthur Keep, scored better on take-off, and the Antelope, flown by Harry Hawker, had a shorter landing run. Hawker later stalled the Antelope effectively placing the Seely in second place after the Limousine.

Converted into a Jupiter test-bed in 1923, the aircraft was later purchased by the Air Ministry and serialled J7004. Fitted with a 435hp Jupiter III driving a two-blade Leitner-Watts propeller, the Seely, (redesignated as the Mk II) thanks to a supercharger, regularly climbed to 23,000ft. The Seely Mk II served the RAE at Farnborough from January 25 until 16 May 1924 but was returned to Bristol in July and dismantled at Filton in December 1924.

| Technical data – Seely | |
|---|---|
| ENGINE | One 240hp Siddeley Puma, one 435hp Bristol Jupiter III with RAE supercharger |
| WINGSPAN | 47ft 3in |
| LENGTH | (Puma) 29ft 6in; (Jupiter) 28ft |
| HEIGHT | 12ft |
| WING AREA | 566sq ft |
| EMPTY WEIGHT | 2,000lb |
| ALL-UP WEIGHT | (Puma) 3,000lb; (Jupiter) 3,600lb |
| MAX SPEED | (Puma) 110mph at sea level; (Jupiter) 121mph at sea level, 137mph at 10,000ft |
| CEILING | (Puma) 18,000ft; (Jupiter) 24,000ft |

**Bristol Seely G-EAUE at Filton in July 1920 just weeks before it was sent to Martlesham Heath. Note the raised rear decking and rear passenger's hatch in the open position.**

# Ten-Seater and Brandon

## Development
In February 1919, Bristol began to consider projects involving passenger and/or cargo-carrying aircraft. Frank Barnwell made several enquiries with potential customers, none of whom were specific about the type of aircraft they needed. Barnwell set to work designing a series of civilian machines capable of carrying up to four passengers in comfort and named the Grampus. In January 1921, the British Treasury opted to inject money into the fledgling air transport industry effectively giving Barnwell the opportunity to start afresh with a new, larger airliner, assisted by W T Reid.

## Design
The Type 62 Ten-Seater was originally designed as a six-passenger aircraft, with a crew of two, powered by a single 400hp Liberty engine. The passengers would be accommodated in a roomy cabin, while the pilot and wireless operator were housed in an open cockpit in front of the upper leading edge. The undercarriage, inherited from the Braemer, was a four-wheel arrangement in tandem with the rear pair fitted with brakes. Later, the design was enlarged to accommodate nine passengers and a pilot with power provided by a 450hp Napier Lion.

The second aircraft, the Type 75, was fitted with a 425hp Jupiter V while the Type 79, named Brandon, was built as a troop-carrier and air ambulance. It was heavily modified compared to the original aircraft. The Brandon featured larger chord wings, Frise ailerons and a ventilated cabin for tropical operations.

## Service
The first aircraft, G-EAWY, made its maiden flight on 21 June 1921 and was in experimental service from Croydon by the following month. After a spell at the Aircraft and Armament Experimental Establishment (A&AEE) at Martlesham Heath, the aircraft was purchased by the Air Council and later served with Instone Air Line and Handley Page Transport. The Type 75, registered as G-EBEV, first flew in June 1922 and was later purchased by Instone in February 1924. By mid-1924, Instone was absorbed into Imperial Airways and the Ten-Seater was converted into a freighter capable of carrying up to 1,800lb. G-EBEV remained part of the Imperial Airways reserve fleet until 1926.

The Brandon made its first flight on 19 March 1924 and was delivered to the RAF on 22 May 1925. Serialled J6997, the Brandon was found to be overweight and did not go into service overseas as planned, but it did serve, alongside the Avro Andover, from Halton, Cheshire, as an air ambulance until January 1926.

## Production
Just four aircraft were built in total, made up of one Type 62 Ten-Seater (G-EAWY, No. 6124); two Type 75 Ten-Seaters (G-EBEV*, No. 6146, and No. 6147, although the latter was never completed and was sold for spares) and one Type 79 Brandon (J6997, No. 6146).

* G-EBEV was redesignated as a Type 75A Express Freight Carrier.

| Technical data – Ten-Seater, Brandon | |
|---|---|
| ENGINE | (Ten-Seater) One 450hp Napier Lion; (Ten-Seater and Brandon) one 425hp Bristol Jupiter IV |
| WINGSPAN | (Ten-Seater) 54ft 3in and 56ft; (Brandon) 54ft 1in |
| LENGTH | (Ten-Seater) 42ft and 40ft 6in; (Brandon) 42ft 3in |
| HEIGHT | (Ten-Seater) 11ft; (Brandon) 14ft 4in |
| WING AREA | (Ten-Seater) 685sq ft and 700sq ft; (Brandon) 890sq ft |
| EMPTY WEIGHT | (Ten-Seater) 3,900lb and 4,000lb; (Brandon) 4,370lb |
| ALL-UP WEIGHT | (Ten-Seater) 6,800lb and 6,755lb; (Brandon) 7,100lb |
| MAX SPEED | (Ten-Seater) 122mph and 100mph; (Brandon) 115mph |
| CEILING | (Ten-Seater) 14,000ft and 8,500ft; (Brandon) 8,500ft |
| ENDURANCE | 5½hrs |
| ACCOMMODATION | Two crew and eight passengers |

**Ten-seater, G-EBEV, after being converted to a freight carrier wearing its RAF Display number '7' at Hendon, London, in 1925. Renamed 'The Express Freight Carrier', the aircraft operated as part of the Imperial Airways reserve fleet until 1926.**

# Bullfinch

## Development
When Bristol acquired the Cosmos Engineering Company, including full rights to the design of the Jupiter engine, Frank Barnwell set about designing a new aircraft to establish the best wing section and fuselage profile most suited to the powerplant. The aircraft, designated the MFA, was a single-seat, all-metal cantilever monoplane that could be converted into a two-seat reconnaissance biplane, with the designation MFB. Interest was shown in the project by the Air Ministry, which drafted specification 2/21 around the two designs and, under Contract No. 114298/21, dated 21 June 1921, placed an order for three prototypes.

## Design
The first two aircraft were built as the Bullfinch Mk I (Type 52), with a wooden parasol wing mounted above an all-metal, carbon steel, drawn tube construction fuselage, braced by tie-rods. The forward fuselage was faired to match the shape of the Jupiter cowling as far back as the pilot's seat. Towards the tail unit, the fuselage was tapered and made up of four longerons covered in flat-sided fabric panels.

The Bullfinch Mk II (Type 53) had a self-contained gunner's cockpit fitted aft of the pilot's, complete with a Scarff ring. A second cantilever wing was mounted directly below the gunner's cockpit and served to move the centre of pressure, compensating for the change in the centre of gravity caused by

The second of only two Bullfinch Mk I monoplanes built, J6902, during its service with the RAE at Farnborough in August 1924.

the additional crew position. A slight re-positioning of the main undercarriage rearwards was the only other difference between the monoplane and biplane variants.

## Production

Three aircraft were built; two prototype Monoplanes (MFA) serialled J6901 and J6902 (No. 6125 and 6126) and a single Biplane (MFB) prototype serialled J6903 (No. 6127).

| Technical data – Bullfinch Monoplane and Biplane | |
|---|---|
| ENGINE | One 425hp Bristol Jupiter III or IV |
| WINGSPAN | 38ft 5in |
| LENGTH | (Monoplane) 24ft 5in; (Biplane) 27ft 6in |
| HEIGHT | 10ft 9in |
| WING AREA | (Monoplane) 267sq ft; (Biplane) 391sq ft |
| EMPTY WEIGHT | (Monoplane) 2,175lb; (Biplane) 2,495lb |
| ALL-UP WEIGHT | (Monoplane) 3,205lb; (Biplane) 4,088lb |
| MAX SPEED | (Monoplane) 135mph at 10,000ft; (Biplane) 120mph at 10,000ft |
| CEILING | (Monoplane) 22,000ft; (Biplane) 18,000ft |
| ENDURANCE | 4hrs |

# M.1D

## Development
Back in 1919, Bristol bought a single M.1B and three M.1Cs back from the Aircraft Disposal Board. All were reconditioned with the intention of selling them as sporting single-seaters, but there was no ready market in post-war Britain. Of these four aircraft, one was shipped direct to New York, while the remainder were registered as G-EASR, G-EAVO and G-EAVP. G-EAVO was sold to a Spanish customer, while G-EASR was retained by Bristol as a demonstrator until early 1925. This left G-EAVP to be converted into the sole M.1D.

## Design
In January 1922, G-EAVP was converted to take a 100hp Bristol Lucifer three-cylinder, air-cooled radial engine; a unit mass produced for the Avro 504K. Redesignated the M.1D, the little aircraft was hard to miss in its scarlet paintwork, black nose and tail, and vivid white lettering.

The trainer variant of the Bulldog – designated the 'TM' – was a two-seat, dual-controlled advanced aircraft. The tail was redesigned and the upper mainplane was swept by 3.5 degrees. Designed to specification T.12/32, the prototype TM, K2188 was first evaluated by the CFS in December 1932.

## Service
The M.1D made its first public appearance at Croydon on 17 April 1922 in the hands of Uwins. In the first race of the day, which was 16 miles long, the M.1D came third and in the second race, which was twice the distance, the aircraft came second having achieved an average speed of more than 100mph. Uwins also took part in the Croydon Whitsun meeting on 3 June, winning the Handicap Race with a higher average speed. On 7 August, with Larry Carter at the controls, G-EAVP won the Aerial Derby Handicap in an average speed of almost 108mph. In September, the M.1D was entered into the King's Cup Race by Rollo de Haga Haig but had to retire after force-landing near Aylesbury, Buckinghamshire, with engine trouble.

The M.1D's next and final public appearance was during the Grosvenor Cup Race on 23 June 1923. There were only nine starters; the M.1D, flown by Maj Leslie Foot was the favourite to win because a higher tuned 140hp Lucifer engine had by then been installed. He was a highly respected and competent pilot who joined Bristol as a staff pilot in April 1923. More than 25,000 spectators had gathered at Filton for the race, which ran from Lympne in Kent via Croydon, Birmingham, Bristol, Croydon and Lympne. Foot was making good progress when he arrived at Filton but complained of petrol fumes, which were coming from a cracked fuel tank. The tank was patched up but while low and at full throttle over Fox Hills near Chertsey, the M.1D dived into the ground and burst into flames. As a mark of respect, Bristol withdrew all its entries for that year's Aerial Derby and King's Cup.

| Technical data – M.1D | |
|---|---|
| ENGINE | One 100hp Bristol Lucifer; One 140hp Lucifer |
| WINGSPAN | 30ft 9in |
| LENGTH | 20ft 4in |
| HEIGHT | 7ft 9in |
| WING AREA | 145sq ft |
| EMPTY WEIGHT | 950lb |
| ALL-UP WEIGHT | 1,300lb |
| MAX SPEED | 125mph |
| CEILING | 22,000ft |
| ENDURANCE | 1¾hrs |

*Above*: The sole Bristol M.1D at Filton, prior to its first public appearance at Croydon in April 1922.

*Right*: Originally built as an M.1C and registered as G-EAVP in September 1920, the M.1D was converted to take an 100hp Lucifer engine in January 1922.

# Racer

## Development

In December 1921, the Napier Lion-powered Gloster Mars I had secured the British speed record at 196.4mph. Roy Fedden, company engineer, was very keen for the Bristol Jupiter to emulate the Lion's success but was frustrated that his requests to build a suitable aircraft to take on the record were not approved. Frank Barnwell had been convinced that the Bullet was adequate for the task and, following his resignation, Fedden and Wilfrid Reid were in a position to design a new high-speed monoplane.

## Design

The Racer was a mid to low-wing monoplane with a rotund low-drag circular-section fuselage. A 510hp Jupiter was fully enclosed, although it was tuned to produce 485hp at 1,850rpm. The wings were un-tapered and fabric-covered and at first were unbraced. The rear fuselage was a monocoque made up of three layers of tulip-wood veneer, while the cantilever tail unit could have its incidence adjusted by a screw-jack. The undercarriage was retractable by using a combination of chains and sprocket gears and, once up, the wheels lay flush in bays and the curved chassis tubes fitted neatly into grooves on the underside of the wing.

## Service

The Type 72 Racer was registered as G-EBDR on 26 June 1922 and was ready for its maiden flight by early July. Finished in bright red, the Racer was striking in appearance, but as soon as Cyril Uwins took-off for the first time, he found the machine to be very tricky to handle. The full-span ailerons were far too powerful, causing the short wings to distort and create severe lateral instability. Uwins did well to get the Racer safely back on the ground after completing a very wide and low circuit of Bristol.

The second flight was no less demanding although the wing situation was slightly improved by wire bracing. Moments after take-off, the larger spinner disintegrated resulting in another delicate circuit by Uwins. It was later discovered that the several layers of heavy paint that had been applied to the spinner were enough extra weight to cause it to fail. The third flight was carried out without a spinner and on this flight the aircraft seemed to behave but the extra drag limited the speed of the racer. The over-zealous ailerons still made the aircraft difficult to handle.

The aileron problem was tackled by installing a cam at the base of the control column so that when it was moved only a similar small movement of the aileron would take place. Movement would progressively increase as the control column was moved further. This system worked perfectly on the ground but, once in the air, the air pressure on the ailerons pushed the face of the cam away from the control column, resulting in virtually no lateral control whatsoever. The only practical solution was to reduce the size of the ailerons by 40 percent and, at the same time, the spinner was replaced with a non-rotating fairing.

A total of seven flights were made, with the final four less alarming for Uwins. Despite the Racer being a very advanced concept, the aircraft was a failure and was scrapped in 1924.

| Technical data – Racer | |
|---|---|
| ENGINE | One 510hp Bristol Jupiter |
| WINGSPAN | 25ft 2in |
| LENGTH | 21ft 7in |
| HEIGHT | 8ft 9in |
| WING AREA | 160sq ft |
| MAX SPEED | 220mph (estimated) |

A remarkable aircraft from any angle, the Type 72 Racer was an advanced design for the early 1920s. It made only seven flights before it was scrapped at Filton in 1924.

# Taxiplane and Primary Trainer

## Development
Frank Barnwell made use of the Cosmos Lucifer for the first time in the design of the Colonial three-seater, which was later abandoned in favour of the Tourer series of biplanes. However, continual development of the Lucifer brought a revival of interest and in July 1921 Barnwell had finished a new aircraft design.

## Design
Design and development of the new aircraft designated the Taxiplane (Type 73) was taken over by Wilfrid Reid when Barnwell emigrated to Australia in October 1921. In February 1922, the Lucifer achieved 'type approval' and was selected to power three Taxiplane prototypes. Of all-wood construction, the Taxiplane was covered in plywood and fabric with identical upper and lower mainplanes that were interchangeable. The Lucifer engine was hinge-mounted to help with maintenance. The aircraft could carry two passengers in a side-by-side cockpit behind the pilots. The passengers accessed the fuselage by a hinged side door on the port side of the aircraft instead of a ladder.

Interest in a two-seat trainer version gained momentum and was given the designation Type 83A Lucifer or Trainer (later known as the PTM). The fuselage was redesigned to accommodate two cockpits in tandem while the same wings, undercarriage and tail unit were retained from the Taxiplane. A later version, the Type 83B, was powered by a 120hp Lucifer IV engine. The final variant, the Type 83E, was substantially strengthened and used as a test bed for the 250hp Bristol Titan five-cylinder radial.

## Service
The first Taxiplane, G-EBEW, made its maiden flight on 22 November 1922 and its first public appearance the following month at the Paris Salon. By April, G-EBEW was being trialled at the A&AEE, proving to be overweight as a three-seater but acceptable as a two-seater. In the meantime, the first of the better performing Trainers, G-EBFZ, was entered into the Grosvenor Race Cup on 23 June 1923, but pilot Uwins was forced to retire with a leaking oil tank.

Six Trainers served with the Filton Reserve Flying School and one was sold to the Bulgarian government. A dozen Type 83B PTMs were sold to Chile, delivered in February and March 1926; another five were delivered to Hungary in April 1926. The sole Type 83E, G-EBYT, was entered into the 1928 King's Cup Race and flown by Sqn Ldr AG Jones-Williams, who averaged a respectable 123mph on the second day leg from Renfrew, Scotland to Lympne, Cheshire.

## Production
A total of 28 aircraft were built, comprising three Taxiplanes, 24 Lucifer PTMs and a single Type 83E (Titan).

| Technical data – Taxiplane, PTM Lucifer and Titan | |
|---|---|
| ENGINE | (Taxi) One 120–140hp Bristol Lucifer; (Trainer) one 120–140hp Lucifer or 220hp Bristol Titan |
| WINGSPAN | 34ft 1in |
| LENGTH | (Taxi) 23ft 3in; (PTM-Lucifer) 24ft 4in; (Trainer-Titan) 25ft 6in |
| HEIGHT | (Taxi and PTM-Lucifer) 8ft 10in; (Trainer-Titan) 9ft 3in |
| EMPTY WEIGHT | (Taxi) 1,210lb; (PTM-Lucifer) 1,340lb; (Trainer-Titan) 1,400lb |
| ALL-UP WEIGHT | (Taxi) 1,840lb; (PTM-Lucifer) 1,900lb; (Trainer-Titan) 2,000lb |
| MAX SPEED | (Taxi) 90mph; (PTM-Lucifer) 96mph; (Trainer-Titan) 130mph |
| ACCOMMODATION | (Taxi) Three; (Trainers) two |

Registered as G-EBEW on 22 November 1922, this prototype Taxiplane made its maiden flight from Filton on 13 February 1923.

# Bloodhound

## Development
By late 1921, a potential replacement for the Bristol F.2 Fighter was in discussion, although that aircraft would remain in service throughout the 1920s, providing Bristol with regular maintenance and reconditioning work. In 1922, the Air Ministry issued specification 3/22 for a two-seat fighter and it was to this criterion that designs for a biplane (Fighter 'C') and a monoplane (Fighter 'D') were submitted in July 1922.

## Design
In February 1923, the Fighter 'C' was named Bloodhound, it was a two-seater biplane with swept two-bay wings and power provided by a Jupiter IV engine. The first aircraft was built as a private venture at the same time as the Air Council invited quotes for three prototype biplanes, one to be all-metal and two with wooden wings and tailplane.

In April 1923, instructions to proceed with the construction of three Bloodhounds for the RAF were received and, in October, Barnwell was back at the helm following his spell in Australia. Barnwell modified the original Bloodhound's engine mounting to adjust the thrust-line and increased the dihedral of the wings, the former improved the pilot's view and the latter solved the prototype's instability problems. The first RAF Bloodhound was all-metal and fitted with a standard Jupiter IV engine, the other two had wooden wings and tail. The second machine had Jupiter IV engine with a variable timing gear for consistent power to 10,000ft, while the third aircraft also had Jupiter IV, but was fitted with an RAE supercharger. All Bloodhounds were fitted with a single fixed forward firing 0.303in Vickers and one 0.303in Lewis machine-gun; the latter was mounted on a Scarff ring in the rear cockpit.

## Service
The private-venture Bloodhound, registered as G-EBGG, first flew in May 1923 and, following Barnwell's improvements was flown to Martlesham Heath on 21 January 1924. The first RAF Bloodhound to fly was the all-metal J7248 on 4 February 1925 and within a month began trials with the A&AEE. Of the two wooden machines, J7236 joined the A&AEE on 22 June and J7237 the RAE on 8 August 1925. All three aircraft were tested and only J7248 suffered a mechanical failure when its metal wing ribs collapsed in the upper centre-plane.

On return from the A&AEE, G-EBGG was overhauled and flown in the 1925 King's Cup Air Race and, in 1926, in a demonstration to prove the reliability of the Jupiter engine, the Bloodhound flew from Croydon to Cairo and back in 56 hours, a distance of 5,400miles.

## Production
Only four Bloodhounds were built, G-EBGG (No. 6222), J7236 and J7237 (No. 6710 and 6711) ordered to Contract No. 389319/22 dated 12 July 1923 and J7248 (No. 6709), which was added to the same contract at a later date.

| Technical data – Bloodhound | |
|---|---|
| ENGINE | One 425hp Bristol Jupiter IV, IV (V.T.) or IV (S/c); one 450hp Jupiter VI or 485hp Jupiter VIII |
| WINGSPAN | 40ft 2in |
| LENGTH | 26ft 6in |
| HEIGHT | 10ft 8in |
| WING AREA | 494sq ft |
| EMPTY WEIGHT | 2,525lb |
| ALL-UP WEIGHT | 4,236lb |
| MAX SPEED | 130mph |
| CEILING | 22,000ft |

Originally designated the 'Fighter 'C'', the Bloodhound was registered as G-EBGG on 3 May 1923.

# Jupiter-Fighter and Advanced Trainers

## Development
Not wishing to spend a great deal of time and money developing a new aircraft, Bristol decided that the quickest way to demonstrate the Jupiter engine was to install it into a spare F.2B airframe. Wilfrid Reid investigated the feasibility and, in early 1923, the company allowed one F.2B (No. 6379) to be converted.

## Design
The Jupiter conversion was straightforward. The airframe remained standard except for some strengthening around the forward fuselage and the fitment of an oleo undercarriage rather than a rubber chord one.

The prototype, designated the Type 76, was completed in April 1923 and at the same time a second and third conversion were sanctioned. The second was designated the Type 76B and was equipped with Frise ailerons. It was renamed the Swedish Fighter after its ultimate owner. The third Jupiter-Fighter was the Type 76A, which was fitted with a high-compression Jupiter engine with a bi-fuel system and gravity fuel tank. The aircraft took off on alcohol and once it was at altitude switched to petrol; this was achieved by fitting two carburettors to the Jupiter engine.

The first of two production variants was the Type 89 trainer and the Type 89A trainer (aka 'Advanced Trainers'); the latter featured a plywood-covered monocoque fuselage, Frise ailerons, and a bigger horn-balanced rudder to check the torque produced by the 320hp Jupiter IV or VI engine.

## Service
Registered as G-EBGF, the Type 76 prototype was first flown by Wg Cdr Norman Macmillan in early June 1923. The second aircraft, G-EBHF, was exhibited at the Göteburg International Aero Exhibition in July 1923 and later sold to the Swedish Air Force. This aircraft remained in military service until 1935 only to be wrecked in civilian hands the following year.

The Jupiter-powered Advanced Trainers saw service with the Reserve Flying School at Filton from 1924 and the Beardmore-operated Reserve Flying School at Renfrew. The type remained in service at Renfrew until 1928 and at Filton until 1933.

## Production
Three Jupiter-Fighters (Type 76, 76A and 76B), nine Trainers (Type 89) and 14 Trainers (Type 89 and 89A) were built.

## Jupiter-Fighter and Advanced Trainers

| Technical data – Jupiter-Fighter and Trainer | |
|---|---|
| ENGINE | (Fighter) One 425hp Bristol Jupiter IV; (Trainer) one 320hp Jupiter VI (DR) or VI (DR) |
| WINGSPAN | 39ft 3in |
| LENGTH | 25ft |
| HEIGHT | 9ft 6in |
| WING AREA | 405sq ft |
| EMPTY WEIGHT | (Fighter) 2,190lb; (Trainer) 2,326lb |
| ALL-UP WEIGHT | (Fighter) 3,080lb; (Trainer) 3,250lb |
| MAX SPEED | (Fighter) 134mph; (Trainer) 110mph |
| CEILING | (Fighter) 22,000ft |
| RANGE | (Fighter) 400 miles; (Trainer) 340 miles |

The first Jupiter-Fighter, G-EBGF, was completed in April 1923, registered in May and flown for the first time by Wg Cdr Norman Macmillan in early June.

# Brownie

## Development
Following the success of the single-seat light-plane competition at Lympne in 1923, the Air Council decided to repeat the event. The 1924 competition would be for two-seat, ultra-light aeroplanes powered by 1,000cc engines.

## Design
Coincidentally, the Bristol Aero Engine Department had been working on a new 30hp Cherub engine, which was a lighter version of the air-cooled, flat twin originally developed for industrial use.

Frank Barnwell produced two designs, both using the Cherub engine. One was made of wood, and the other, an all-metal construction, was initially designated the Type 91 Brownie. Two more aircraft were authorised on 4 February and 5 May 1923. All had identical fuselages made from steel tubing covered in fabric, but all of the Brownies had different wings. The prototype was fitted with wooden wings. The second aircraft built was fitted with longer-span metal wings, while the third machine had a long-range fuel tank installed and shorter-span metal wings.

The first aircraft was later fitted with a 36hp Cherub III engine, mounted lower in the nose and combined with new longerons sloping from the rear cockpit towards the nose, to improve the pilot's forward visibility. It was also fitted with metal wings and a larger fuel tank and redesignated the Type 91A. The fuselage was revised yet again on the prototype with an even lower thrust line, horn-balanced rudder, new undercarriage and a Fairey-Reed duralumin propeller and redesignated again to the Type 91B Brownie II.

## Service
The prototype, G-EBJK, was first flown by Uwins on 6 August 1924 and, despite a crash landing at Filton on 5 September, it was quickly repaired and finished second in the Lympne Air Council trials held

After steel wings and a larger fuel tank were installed, G-EBJK, redesignated the Brownie, named *Brownie Jack*, to a Type 91A. The other two aircraft were named *Jill* and *Jim*.

between 27 September and 4 October. The second aircraft, G-EBJL, flew for the first time just five days before the Lympne trials started and had to be withdrawn because of aileron flutter. The third aircraft, G-EBJM, first flew on 24 September just in time to take third place in the Grosvenor Trophy race.

G-EBJK was later evaluated at the A&AEE as a potential primary trainer in its original form and again with the Cherub III engine and metal wings but was rejected on both occasions. As the Type 91B Brownie II, G-EBJK took third prize in the Daily Mail trials held at Lympne in 1926 with Uwins at the controls. G-EBJK was destroyed in an accident in March 1928, while the two surviving Brownies served out their days with the Wessex Aeroplane Club and the London Aeroplane Club.

## Production

Three Brownies were built, G-EBJK (Type 91, modified to Type 91A and again to 91B (No. 6526)), G-EBJL (Type 91A (No. 6527)) and Mk II, G-EBJM (Type 91B (No. 6528)).

| Technical data – Brownie | |
|---|---|
| ENGINE | One 32hp Bristol Cherub I or one 36hp Cherub III |
| WINGSPAN | (91 wood) 34ft 7in; (91 metal) 36ft 7in; (91 single-seat) 30ft 7in; (91A and B) 37ft 7in |
| LENGTH | 26ft 3in |
| HEIGHT | 6ft 6in |
| WING AREA | (91 wood) 204sq ft; (91 metal) 208sq ft; (91 single-seat) 172sq ft; (91A and B) 210sq ft |
| EMPTY WEIGHT | (91) 500lb; (91A and B) 690lb |
| ALL-UP WEIGHT | (91) 870lb; (91 single-seat) 720lb; (91A and B) 1,010lb |
| MAX SPEED | (91 and 91A) 70mph; (91B) 78mph |
| RANGE | (91) 100 miles; (91A and B) 125 miles |

# Berkeley

## Development
Bristol was among several aircraft manufacturers invited to tender for Specification 26/2.3 which called for a two-seat long-range day bomber. Designs were also presented by Handley Page, Hawker and Westland for the bomber, all of which were powered by the Rolls-Royce liquid-cooled engine.

## Design
The initial design of the aircraft, known as the Type 90 Berkeley from October 1923, was produced by Wilfrid T Reid, assisted by Clifford Tinson, who had just joined the company from Avro. It was Tinson who suggested the introduction of a Type number system to Bristol, copying the method that was used by Avro.

The Berkeley was an all-metal, fabric-covered aircraft, with equal-span biplane mainplanes and a specified Condor engine mounted in the nose. The pilot was positioned in front of the leading edge of the upper mainplane, while the gunner/observer was located in the upper rear fuselage. The latter position had a Scarff-ring for a single 0.303in Lewis machine gun and below and forward was a cabin, which had a prone bomb aimer's position in the floor.

Very similar in appearance to the Avro Aldershot and built in the same way structurally as the Bloodhound, the Berkeley was finished on paper when Reid resigned from the company. Frank Barnwell took over as chief designer and altered the design by extending the rear fuselage, relocating the radiators and making the fin and rudder taller. However, once the mock-up was viewed by Air Ministry officials in January 1924, the radiator was relocated to its original position in the nose.

## Service
Encouraged by the Air Ministry, the first Berkeley, J7403, was requested with a completion date of August 1924 and, along with the second aircraft, J7404 would be accepted with wooden wings and tailplane to help speed up delivery. However, the first aircraft was not ready on time and even then was only in skeletal form until November. Following the fitment of stronger rear longerons, it did not make its first flight until 5 March 1925. Only the third aircraft, J7405 was built as intended with all-metal wings and fuselage, but this did not fly until 11 February 1926.

J7403 arrived at the A&AEE, Martlesham Heath, in late March 1925 and performed reasonably well against the Handcross, Yeovil and Horsley. However, along with the Handcross, the Berkeley was viewed as better suited for night bombing, which immediately put both aircraft out of the running because a policy change had been implemented which prevented single-engine aircraft from being used for night operations. As a result, the Horsley won a production order and all three Berkeleys were relegated to experimental flying with the RAE. Both J7404 and J7405 were used for short-wave telephony experiments; the latter flying for the last time on 8 July 1928. This aircraft survived until December 1930 as a ground test rig at Farnborough.

## Production

Three Type 90 Berkeleys were ordered to Contract 445078/23, built to Specification 26/2.3 and serialled J7403–J7405. All were delivered to the A&AEE between March 1925 and June 1926.

| Technical data – Berkeley | |
|---|---|
| ENGINE | One 650hp Rolls-Royce Condor III |
| WINGSPAN | 57ft 11in |
| LENGTH | 47ft 6in |
| HEIGHT | 14ft |
| WING AREA | 985sq ft |
| EMPTY WEIGHT | 5,200lb |
| ALL-UP WEIGHT | 8,128lb |
| MAX SPEED | 120mph |
| ENDURANCE | 12hrs |

Bristol Type 90 Berkeley J7403 was the first of only three built at Filton in late February 1925, shown days before its maiden flight on 5 March. The aircraft enjoyed a short flying career and was scrapped 12 months later.

# Boarhound and Beaver

## Development
With a potential order of at least 90 aircraft still for the taking, enough to re-equip four F.2B Fighter squadrons, Frank Barnwell began a freelance design in response to feedback from test pilots who had flown the Bloodhound. The aircraft was designed around Specification 8/24 for a new army co-operation two-seater to replace the Bristol Fighter.

## Design
The new machine, a two-bay staggered un-swept biplane named Boarhound, had equal-span wings with unequal chords and Frise ailerons fitted to the lower mainplane only. The aircraft was constructed with a new system, developed by Harry Pollard, of tensile steel strips shaped into cusped and flanged sections. These were riveted together lengthways to form struts and longerons to create a structure that was light, strong and considerably cheaper to produce than the drawn tube method. The fuselage was made up of Warren girders in the forward section and was wire-braced towards the rear.

The fuselage was deep so that a large wireless, messaging equipment and a camera could be accommodated. The pilot had a fixed forward firing 0.303in Vickers, the observer had a Scarff ring-mounted 0.303in Lewis machine gun and the Boarhound could carry a pair of 112lb bombs. The aircraft was built in three versions, the prototype, designated Type 93, was a pure army co-operation machine powered by a Jupiter IV, while the Type 93A, named Beaver, was a general-purpose aircraft. The Type 93B, Boarhound II, was powered by a 450hp Jupiter VI and was designed for fighter reconnaissance.

## Service
The first Boarhound Mk 1, registered as G-EBLG on 28 May 1925, carried out its maiden flight on 8 June. The aircraft was entered into official trials at Martlesham Heath on 10 August, in competition with the Armstrong Whitworth Atlas, which proved to be superior.

In the meantime, a new requirement for the DH.9A replacement was issued and Bristol was still convinced that the Boarhound stood a chance. Redesigned and re-engined, a second prototype emerged as the Beaver Mk I. Registered G-EBQF, Uwins first flew the general-purpose machine on 23 February 1927. Again though, Bristol lost out, this time to the Fairey IIIF.

In late 1925, Chile expressed an interest in the Boarhound and once modified into a two-seat fighter-bomber, the design re-appeared with the name Borzoi. The proposal was unsuccessful although two aircraft were ordered by Mexico under the name Boarhound Mk II along with ten new Bristol Fighters.

## Production
Four aircraft were built; one Boarhound Mk I (No. 6805 (Type 93)), one Beaver (No. 7123 (Type 93A)) and two Boarhound Mk IIs (Nos. 7232 and 7233 (Type 93B)).

| Technical data – Boarhound I (93), II (93B) and Beaver (93A) | |
|---|---|
| ENGINE | One 425hp Bristol Jupiter IV or one 450hp Jupiter VI |
| WINGSPAN | 44ft 9in |
| LENGTH | 31ft 6in |
| HEIGHT | 11ft 8in |
| WING AREA | 464sq ft |
| EMPTY WEIGHT | (93) 2,900lb; (93A) 2,906lb; (93B) 3,000lb |
| ALL-UP WEIGHT | (93) 4,460lb; (93A) 4,480lb; (93B) 4,500lb |
| MAX SPEED | (93) 135mph; (93A) 142mph; (93B) 140mph |
| CEILING | 22,000ft |
| ENDURANCE | 3hrs |

**The Boarhound Mk I, G-EBLG, pictured at Martlesham Heath in November 1925 with a 450hp Jupiter VI engine installed.**

# Type 92

## Development
The question of how to keep a fully cowled radial engine cool in flight plagued Bristol and the aviation industry as a whole during the mid-1920s. The Jupiter, in particular, proved difficult to keep cool in the Badger, Bullfinch and Ten-seater despite the promise shown by wind-tunnel models. To help solve this problem, Frank Barnwell with the backing of Roy Fedden, proposed the construction of a full-scale biplane in January 1924, with a circular, slim fuselage that was basically a scaled-up version of a wind-tunnel model.

## Design
The idea was put to the Air Ministry which, in April 1924, issued a research contract that covered the cost of the manufacture and testing of a single aircraft. On April 17 of that year, Barnwell presented a general arrangement drawing of a two-bay, equal-span biplane with a slender fuselage and large, 9ft gap between each mainplane. The latter feature was designed to cause as little aerodynamic interaction between the wings and fuselage as possible and, coupled with a very wide-track undercarriage, made the aircraft look very ungainly.

The fuselage was a simple design made up of box girder covered in plywood with a square cross section to the rear of the second cockpit and tapering to the tail unit. The latter, like the wings, was of a rectangular design with squared-off tips made up of fabric-covered steel strip and tube.

## Service
Fitted with a Jupiter VI nine-cylinder air-cooled radial, (on loan from the Air Ministry) the sole Type 92 (No. 6920) carried out its maiden flight from Filton on 13 November 1925. Not only was the Type 92, also known as the 'Laboratory' biplane, an unattractive machine, it was also sluggish to fly, which was attributable to the large gap between the wings that equated to 25 percent of the wingspan.

Initial flight testing, carried out in the vicinity of Filton, was performed with a 3ft-diameter fuselage, but the un-tapered section of the fuselage was designed to accommodate five different diameter fairings to test the aerodynamic effects of an exposed radial and a fully enclosed one. It was only from 1928 that the larger 5ft-fairing was fitted, which fully enclosed the 4ft 7in diameter Jupiter engine. However, not long after, the Type 92's undercarriage collapsed during a heavy landing and the machine never flew again.

It is not clear how much the Type 92 contributed to the problem of cooling radials but, in 1929, the Townend ring first appeared and the solution was found.

**The Type 92 or 'Laboratory' biplane at Filton before the 450hp Bristol Jupiter VI was installed.**

# Badminton

## Development
Roy Fedden was determined to prove how good an engine the Bristol Jupiter was, especially when compared to the Armstrong Siddeley Jaguar. Fedden was also a great advocate of using aircraft powered by the Jupiter to prove their worth by air racing and record breaking. Following the death of Major Leslie Foot in 1923, the directors of the company had put a stop to such activities, much to the chagrin of Fedden, who persevered until Frank Barnwell was allowed to design a new racing aircraft in September 1925, which was officially approved on October 13.

## Design
The latest Barnwell creation was the Type 99, powered by a Jupiter VI, with a potential top speed of 180mph. A single-seat equal-span biplane, the machine, christened the Badminton, was constructed of wood (mainly spruce) and steel tube and covered in fabric. The fuselage was very streamlined, being at no point greater in diameter than the Jupiter engine and in its original form, even the engine's cylinder heads were shrouded in special aerodynamic 'helmets'.

The wings had a very thin section with spars made of spruce and ailerons only fitted on the lower mainplane. The upper mainplane was connected to the upper fuselage by a streamlined pylon, while the lower set of wings were separated by a 4ft 6in section that also carried the undercarriage.

The wings were subject to change on three further occasions, beginning with the raising of the upper mainplane on four struts and an increase in span by 2ft 6in to 26ft 7in. The next change was a new upper centre section, similar to that already in place in the lower mainplane, which raised the overall span to 28ft 6in. The final change was a new set of 33ft-span wings, which were tapered from root to tip.

## Service
The Badminton first flew on 5 May 1926 with a 510hp Jupiter VI in time for that year's Kings Cup race on 9 July, which would be flown by Imperial Airways Capt Frank Barnard. Favourite to win, Barnard was forced to retire because of a broken fuel line. He wanted to fly the aircraft again in the 1927 race on the condition that several changes were made, which included the fitment of a 440hp Jupiter VII, known as the Orion at the time. The wing modifications already mentioned, were carried out prior to the start of the race. By then, the aircraft had been redesignated as the Type 99A and was powered by a smaller diameter 525hp Jupiter VI.

On 28 July 1927, Barnard carried out a run over the speed course at Filton to help determine the propeller to use for the race. On reaching just 200ft, the engine suddenly seized, forcing Barnard to glide towards a field near Winterbourne. Just as he turned into the wind, and at a height of only 80ft, the aircraft stalled and crashed, killing Barnard outright.

| Technical data – Badminton | |
|---|---|
| ENGINE | (a) One 510hp Bristol Jupiter VI; (b) one 440hp Jupiter VII; (c) one 525hp Jupiter VI (short-stroke) |
| WINGSPAN | (a) 24ft 1in; (b) 26ft 7in; (c) 33ft |
| LENGTH | (a) 21ft 2in; (b and c) 21ft 5in |
| HEIGHT | (a) 9ft 2in; (b and c) 9ft 6in |
| WING AREA | (a) 210sq ft; (b) 221sq ft; (c) 299sq ft |
| EMPTY WEIGHT | (a) 1,770lb; (b and c) 1,800lb |
| ALL-UP WEIGHT | (a) 2,470lb; (b and c) 2,500lb |
| MAX SPEED | 160mph |

Cyril Uwins poses in the cockpit of the sole Badminton, G-EBMK, which made its maiden flight from Filton on 5 May 1926. Note the individual 'helmet' fairings over the Jupiter VIs cylinder heads.

# Bagshot

## Development
In late 1924, the Air Ministry issued Specification F.4/24 for a twin-engine, three-seat fighter (one pilot and a pair of gunners) capable of 125mph and with a landing speed of no greater than 50mph. With no mention of how the aircraft was to be armed, Frank Barnwell produced an all-metal, semi-cantilever wing monoplane design that was accepted by the Air Ministry. A single prototype, at a cost of £14,750, was ordered in March 1925. Bristol came up with the name Bludgeon but was overruled and by July the aircraft had been named Bagshot.

## Design
The Bagshot was an unusual looking aircraft from all angles, beginning with triangular cross-section fuselage made up of a three steel longerons and tubular struts covered in fabric. The wing had a pair of main spars with nose ribs made of duralumin and was also fabric-covered. The undercarriage had such a wide track that the opportunity to fit a pair of aerofoil axle fairings was taken, and these were large enough to contribute to the aircraft's overall lift.

While the design work continued, the Air Ministry instructed in September 1925 that the design should include fitment of supercharged engines, larger fuel tanks and a requirement for a higher top speed at altitude. At the same time, the potential armament was disclosed as being a pair of 37mm Cow guns for use at night against heavy bombers. The new criteria presented to Barnwell showed that Bagshot would be overweight and the landing speed too high. Despite suggesting that the project should be abandoned, the Air Ministry refused to cancel the contract and the sole aircraft, serialled J7767 (No. 7018), was duly accepted with a pair of non-supercharged Jupiter VI engines on 12 May 1927.

## Service
The Bagshot was flown by Uwins on 15 July 1927 without problem. However, as flight trials proceeded and higher speeds were explored, it was discovered that lateral control quickly deteriorated because of flexing in the wing. A lengthy programme of structural testing saw Barnwell admitting defeat to the point where he suggested that the aircraft should be redesigned as a biplane. This would mean starting the whole project again and the Bagshot did not fly again. However, the information gleaned from the exercise was used by the Air Ministry in 1928 to investigate the torsional stiffness of cantilever wings. This work was continued until the aircraft was scrapped in 1931.

On the surface, the Bagshot design appeared to be a disaster, but while the Air Ministry was carrying out its studies, a contract was awarded to Harold Pollard to build and test his own design for a multi-spar wing. This successful exercise resulted in a later order for the multi-engine troop carrier, which evolved into the Bombay.

| Technical data – Bagshot | |
|---|---|
| ENGINE | Two 450hp Bristol Jupiter VI |
| WINGSPAN | 70ft |
| LENGTH | 44ft 1in |
| HEIGHT | 9ft 6in |
| WING AREA | 840sq ft |
| EMPTY WEIGHT | 5,100lb |
| ALL-UP WEIGHT | 8,195lb |
| MAX SPEED | 125mph |
| ARMAMENT (not fitted) | Two Coventry Ordnance 37mm Cow gun |

The one and only Bagshot, J7767, a twin-engined, three-seater fighter, at Filton, around the time of its maiden flight on 15 July 1927.

# Bulldog

## Development
Designed to Air Ministry Specification F.9/26 that called for a replacement for the Siskin and Gamecock in RAF fighter squadrons, the Bulldog was chosen from a group of contenders that included the Goldfinch, Hawfinch, Partridge and Starling.

## Design
One of the classic Frank Barnwell designs, the Bulldog, was an unequal-span, single-bay biplane, with an all-metal, fabric-covered airframe. The aircraft had a variable-incidence tailplane and the tailskid had through-axle main units and compressed rubber shock absorbers. Power for the main production variants, the Mk II and Mk IIA, was a Jupiter VII radial. Service equipment included oxygen and a short-wave radio transmitter and receiver. The Mk IIA was a much stronger aircraft and featured a redesigned undercarriage, bigger tyres, and a modified fin and tailwheel in place of the skid.

A trainer variant of the Bulldog designated the 'TM' (Training Machine) was a two-seat dual-controlled advanced aircraft. The tail was redesigned and the upper mainplane was swept by 3½ degrees. Designed to Specification T.12/32, the prototype TM, K2188, was first evaluated by the CFS (Central Flying School) in December 1932.

## Service
The prototype Bulldog Mk I, J9051, first flew on 17 May 1927 and performed so well that the aircraft was delivered to the A&AEE the following month. In May 1929, the first Bulldog Mk IIs joined 3 Squadron at Upavon, Wiltshire, and made the first significant public debut at that year's Hendon Air Display and would remain a regular performer until 1936. Memorable mock bombing attacks and coloured smoke displays with these aircraft by 19, 3 and 54 squadrons in 1934, 1935 and 1936, respectively, were some of the show highlights.

By 1932, nine RAF squadrons had re-equipped on the type and, up to their retirement, approximately 70 percent of Britain's home-fighter defence were Bulldogs, despite the average speed of light bombers in service being higher. The type never saw action in RAF service, although the Bulldogs of 3 Squadron were mobilised and sent to Sudan during the Abyssinian crisis in 1935 and early 1936.

The RAF received 312 of all Bulldogs built, and they served with 3, 17, 19, 23, 29, 32, 41, 54, 56 and 111 Squadrons. The type also served the Australian, Danish, Estonian, Finnish, Latvian, Siamese and Swedish air forces. The Bulldog saw action with the Finnish Air Force during the Winter War in 1939.

The Bulldog TM entered service with the CFS at Wittering, the RAF College Cranwell, 1 FTS (Flying Training School) Leuchars, 3 FTS Grantham, 4 FTS Egypt and 5 FTS Sealand in 1932 and was withdrawn by 1935.

## Production
In total, 443 Bulldogs were built, comprising one Type 102, two Mk Is, one 'High-Altitude' (conversion), 92 Mk IIs, 268 Mk IIAs, two Mk IIIAs, one Mk IV, 18 Mk IVAs, 59 TMs and a pair of Japanese Single Seat Fighters (JSSFs) built by the Nakajima Aircraft Works in Tokyo.

# Bulldog

| Technical data – Bulldog IIA and TM | |
|---|---|
| ENGINE | (IIA) One 490hp Bristol Jupiter VIIF; one 460hp Jupiter VIF |
| WINGSPAN | 33ft 11in |
| LENGTH | 25ft 2in |
| HEIGHT | 9ft 10in |
| WING AREA | 306sq ft |
| EMPTY WEIGHT | (IIA) 2,412lb; (TM) 2,200lb |
| ALL-UP WEIGHT | (IIA) 3,530lb; (TM) 3,426lb |
| MAX SPEED | (IIA) 174mph at 10,000ft; (TM) 168mph at 28,000ft |
| RATE OF CLIMB | 20,000ft in 14mins 30secs |
| CEILING | (IIA) 27,000ft; (TM) 28,000ft |
| ARMAMENT | Twin 0.303in synchronised Vickers machine guns |

*Right*: The prototype Bristol Bulldog Mk II, J9480 powered by a 440hp Jupiter VII engine, made its maiden flight on 21 January 1928. The Mk II and Mk IIA were the most prolific of all Bulldogs built.

*Below*: The first of 70 Bulldog TMs (Training Machine) built was K2188 and was delivered to the Aeroplane and Armament Experimental Establishment (A&AEE) for evaluation in December 1931. Operated as a two-seat, dual-controlled trainer, the TM gave good service from 1932 to 1935.

32 Squadron, based at Kenley, Surrey, began receiving the Bulldog IIA, in place of the Armstrong Whitworth Siskin Mk IIIA in January 1931. The unit retained the fighter until July 1936 when it was replaced by the Gloster Gauntlet Mk II at Biggin Hill.

# Type 101

## Development
Inspired by Fairey's approach of designing an aircraft for speed (the Fairey Fox), rather than for its ability to carry equipment (an inevitable Air Ministry specification), Frank Barnwell and Roy Fedden designed an aircraft capable of 160mph. Convinced that the Air Ministry would eventually favour high-speed, lightly equipped aircraft, Fedden worried that orders would suddenly come flooding in for machines powered by water-cooled engines with a low frontal area, such as the Fox, rather than the more cumbersome-looking radial. It was time to prove the capability of the radial all over again and, by late 1925, Fedden was already developing a military version of the Mercury engine.

## Design
The Bristol directors approved the construction of a single aircraft as a private venture, hoping that it would generate interest from the Air Ministry. By January 1926, the new project, designated the Type 101, was ready. It had the general arrangement of a fighter, featuring twin front machine guns, two more mounted on the observer's Scarff-ring, 1,200 rounds of ammunition, and could carry up to 70 gallons of fuel, oxygen and parachutes although wireless, bomb equipment and a camera were absent.

The structure used steel for the wings and tail unit while the fuselage was a plywood-covered monocoque with a spruce structure all of which was covered in fabric. Power was intended to come from a 480hp Mercury, but the aircraft would initially use a 450hp Jupiter VI.

## Service
The design was presented to the Air Ministry in March 1926 and was immediately rejected because of the use of wood, which was out of favour compared to all-metal aircraft. As a result, only the prototype was ever built, registered as G-EBOW (No. 7019) on 17 July 1926.

The Type 101 was not completed until July 1927 and first flew on 8 August. It was exhibited in Copenhagen only days later. Despite plenty of interest in the Type 101, no orders materialised. The aircraft proved to be very useful to Bristol, making an excellent test-bed in place of the Badminton.

By the end of 1927, all armament had been removed and, in April 1928, it was decided to make the aircraft as aerodynamic as possible so that it stood a good chance in that year's Kings Cup race. With a Jupiter IVA installed, Cyril Uwins and Arthur Suddes as passenger, flew the Type 101 into second place at an average speed of 159.9mph over the two-day event.

Later fitted with a 485hp Mercury II, the Type 101 was lost on 29 November 1929 when the upper wing centre section failed during an overspeed test. The pilot, CRL Shaw, escaped safely by parachute, becoming only the fourth civilian pilot in Britain to do so and securing his place in the Caterpillar Club.

## Type 101

| Technical data – Type 101 | |
|---|---|
| ENGINE | One 450hp Bristol Jupiter VI or VIA; one 485hp Bristol Mercury II |
| WINGSPAN | 33ft 7in |
| LENGTH | 27ft 4in |
| HEIGHT | 9ft 6in |
| WING AREA | 360sq ft |
| EMPTY WEIGHT | 2,100lb |
| ALL-UP WEIGHT | 3,540lb |
| MAX SPEED | 160mph or racing 170mph |
| CEILING | 21,000ft |

The Bristol Type 101, G-EBOW, as it appeared during the 1928 King's Cup Air Race, sporting racing number '21' on the tail; the aircraft finished a creditable second.

# Type 107 Bullpup

## Development
The story of the Bullpup began in 1924 when Frank Barnwell started work on a Rolls-Royce Falcon-powered fighter, to Specification F.17/24, for a single-seat, high-speed fighter landplane. Bristol was less than enthusiastic, preferring to use its own engines in its own aircraft and this resulted in the design being put on hold until 1926. Barnwell began work on a similar aircraft designated Type 102, which was produced to Specification F.9/26 for a day-and-night fighter and Specification N.21/26 for a naval fleet fighter. Once the design reached the proposal stage, it had evolved into the Type 105, a single-seat fighter powered by a Mercury engine aimed at F.9/26. A pair of mock-ups was inspected by the Air Ministry in February 1927, and resulted in a design revision to a later Specification, F.20/27, which would eventually be contended by the Bulldog and the Hawker Fury, among others. Bristol still considered Barnwell's design worth building as a single prototype.

## Design
The resulting aircraft was designated the Type 107 to be powered by a 480hp Mercury engine. An unequal span single bay biplane, the Bullpup was of all-metal construction, covered in fabric. Like the Bulldog, the structure was made up of high-tensile steel strips riveted together. Armament consisted of a pair of 0.303in Lewis machine-guns positioned at each side of the cockpit.

## Service
Due to a lack of Mercury engines, the sole Bullpup, serialled J9051, first flew with a Jupiter VI engine on 28 April 1928. The aircraft was re-engined with a 480hp Mercury IIA in January 1929 and, in March, was sent to the A&AEE for the first time where it was entered into the F.20/27 interceptor competition.

In early 1930, having failed to impress the Air Ministry, the Bullpup was fitted with a Jupiter VIIF and, following another spell with the A&AEE, made a rare public appearance at Hendon (No. 2) in June 1930. Re-engined again with a Mercury SS in the autumn of 1931, the Bullpup served again with the A&AEE between November 1932 and April 1933 until it was returned to Filton for its final engine change. Re-engined with an Aquila I, the Bullpup successfully carried out a 200hr endurance test between 2 April and 9 May 1935. After appearing at the Society of British Aerospace Companies (SBAC) Display at Hendon on 1 July 1935, the aircraft was transferred to the Bristol Flying School and was retired by the end of the year once the Aquila test programme came to an end.

A useful test-bed, the Bullpup is also believed to have tested the Aquila III and Perseus IA engines.

## Type 107 Bullpup

| Technical data – Type 107 Bullpup | |
|---|---|
| ENGINE | One 450hp Jupiter VI; one 480hp Bristol Mercury IIA; one 440hp Jupiter VIIF; one 400hp Mercury (short-stroke); one 500hp Aquila I; one Aquila III and one 600hp Perseus IA |
| WINGSPAN | 30ft |
| LENGTH | 23ft 6in |
| HEIGHT | 9ft 5in |
| WING AREA | 230sq ft |
| EMPTY WEIGHT | 1,910lb |
| ALL-UP WEIGHT | 2,850lb |
| MAX SPEED | (Mercury IIA) 190mph |

The sole Bristol Bullpup, J9051 (No. 7178) was fitted with four different Bristol radial engines during its career, including 480hp Mercury IIA with a Townend ring. The aircraft is pictured at Filton in May 1929.

# Type 109

## Development
On 22 May 1927, Charles Lindbergh carried out the first solo crossing of the Atlantic from New York to Paris, breaking the RAF's long-distance record from Cranwell to the Persian Gulf set the previous day by a Hawker Horsley. Following two more attempts to beat the record in the Horsley, both of which failed, tenders from the Air Ministry were issued for a specialist long-distance aircraft. Bristol responded with a biplane design and Fairey with a monoplane; the latter was ultimately ordered by the Air Ministry, but Bristol decided to proceed with its aircraft as a private venture.

## Design
Designated the Type 109, the aircraft was an all-metal, single-bay, unstaggered biplane of simplistic design with an enclosed cabin and dual controls for a pair of pilots seated in tandem. The undercarriage was a straightforward cross-axle design and the tailwheel was fitted with a low-pressure tyre. The Jupiter VIII engine was specially tuned for economy and drove a large, four-blade propeller.

## Service
The sole prototype Type 109 was registered as G-EBZK (No. 7268) on 4 July 1928 and was first flown by Cyril Uwins on 7 September. Before the aircraft flew, Bert Hinkler was interested in using it for a flight around the world but, even with a reduced gross weight of 9,800lb, the Type 109 would need too long a take-off run to attempt such a challenge. Use of larger aerodromes at the time would have caused many political problems.

Instead, the Type 109 was used as an engine test-bed for the Jupiter XF engine, which would be fitted into the Handley Page HP.42 and Short Kent, both ordered for Imperial Airways. From May 1929, pilots from Imperial Airways were loaned and Roy Fedden suggested that the aircraft and engine could gain publicity by flying to Australia. However, by 1930, a Jupiter XIF engine had been fitted and a 350hr contract issued to carry out the less glamorous role of flying a 15-hour daily circuit around Britain.

The endurance test commenced from Farnborough on 12 September 1930 with a 'sealed' Jupiter XIF engine and all was well until a rocker tie-rod broke after 260 hours of flying in January 1931. The aircraft force-landed at Lympne. Another 40 hours were flown without incident. Fedden also suggested using the Type 109 for a similar endurance test with the Mercury V engine, but this was later carried out by the Type 118.

Without ever leaving the shores of Britain, the Type 109 was scrapped in late 1931.

## Type 109

| Technical data – Type 109 | |
|---|---|
| ENGINE | One 480hp Bristol Jupiter VIII; one 490hp Jupiter XIF |
| WINGSPAN | 51ft 2in |
| LENGTH | 37ft 9in |
| HEIGHT | 14ft |
| WING AREA | 700sq ft |
| WING LOADING | 17lb per sq/ft |
| EMPTY WEIGHT | 4,600lb |
| ALL-UP WEIGHT | 9,800lb |
| CRUISE SPEED | 90mph |
| MAX RANGE | 3,300 miles |

**Type 109 G-EBZK in its original form with a 480hp Bristol Jupiter VIII engine and original fuel tanks providing the aircraft with a potential range of 3,300 miles.**

# Type 110A

## Development
Frank Barnwell had produced a host of designs for small civil transport aircraft, the majority of which were pitched at Imperial Airways, which rejected them all, mainly on the grounds of economy. The Jupiter engine was not suited to such aircraft, proving to be too large for the smaller passenger machines. However, following the introduction of the smaller five-cylinder Titan in late 1927 and the slightly larger seven-cylinder Neptune engine in September 1928, a more attractive package could be offered at a much-reduced price.

## Design
Barnwell's initial design was for the Titan-powered Type 110, which was revised to the Type 110A in January 1928. The Type 110A could be fitted with either the Titan or Neptune engine, depending on the customer's needs and was capable of carrying four passengers. An all-metal aircraft, the Type 110A, was covered in fabric and had three large windows on each side of the cabin. The cabin was upholstered in blue leather and blue carpet and had excellent ventilation for passengers. The pilot had a good field of view from his fully glazed, enclosed cockpit, which was located in front of the leading edge of the upper mainplane.

One of Bristol's criteria for the aircraft was that it should be presented at a retail price of £3,000 but, when it was determined that even with a healthy production, the actual cost to Bristol was £3,500, the directors of the company decided only to produce two prototypes. As the project fee approached £15,000, with no orders in sight, only one aircraft was built.

## Service
Registered as G-AAFG on 12 March 1929, the aircraft was sufficiently complete (the Neptune engine was a mock-up) to be displayed at the Olympia Show, which was opened by the Prince of Wales on 16 July.

Uwins first flew the Type 110A with a Titan engine from Filton on 25 October 1929 and the aircraft demonstrated promising performance. In early 1930, the aircraft was re-engined with the Neptune engine and flight testing continued satisfactorily until February 1930. On landing on an uneven part of the airfield, G-AAFG began to 'porpoise', causing the upper oleo leg attachments to fail and to be pushed through the floor of the cockpit. Uwins was lucky to escape without serious injury, and this appears to have brought about the demise of the Type 110A, which was not viewed as worth repairing and the aircraft was scrapped not long after.

| Technical data – Type 110A | |
|---|---|
| ENGINE | One 220hp Bristol Titan; one 315hp Neptune |
| WINGSPAN | 40ft 6in |
| LENGTH | 33ft 6in |
| HEIGHT | 10ft 2in |
| WING AREA | 389sq ft |
| EMPTY WEIGHT | 2,330lb |
| ALL-UP WEIGHT | 4,360lb |
| MAX SPEED | 125mph |
| ACCOMMODATION | Pilot and four passengers |

Only two Type 110As were built, the first, G-AAFG, pictured at Filton in January 1930 with a 315hp Neptune installed.

# Type 118 and 120

## Development
Riding on the success of the Bulldog, which was attracting interest from abroad, Bristol designed two-seat, general purpose aircraft for the use of foreign air forces. Designed along the same lines as an overseas general-purpose RAF aircraft such as the DH.9A and Fairey IIID, Barnwell sketched the design of a Jupiter XFA-powered machine in August 1929. In February 1930, the design became the Type 118 and two aircraft were authorised for construction as a private venture.

## Design
The Type 118 was an aerodynamic single-bay biplane with unequal, staggered wings. General construction was similar to the Bulldog; the metal frame being covered by fabric. Crewed by two, the pilot had a single 0.303in synchronised Lewis machine gun, while the observer had a Scarff ring-mounted 0.303in Lewis machine gun. Offensive loads included a pair of 250lb bombs and four 112lb or 16 20lb bombs carried on external racks. The Mercury-powered Type 120 differed by having a cupola for the rear gunner's cockpit complete with transparent panels and a modified Scarff ring.

## Service
Registered as G-ABEZ on 12 September 1930, the Type 118 was first flown by Uwins on 22 January 1931. The experimental marking 'R-3' was applied in the summer of 1931 and, on 30 October, the Type 118 was cleared for airworthiness trials at Martlesham Heath, where it was was well-received and proved pleasant to handle.

A planned demonstration tour to Scandinavia and the Baltic states was disrupted by the Gnome-Rhone company questioning sales rights in certain countries. In the meantime, the Air Ministry were impressed by how the Type 118 had performed at Martlesham and a request to hire the aircraft was placed for Mercury V testing. In February 1932, the aircraft was fitted with this engine, driving a four-blade propeller and serialled K2873. Following trials, which included a lengthy period in the Middle East, the aircraft went into storage until April 1935 and was then used as a test bed for the Pegasus PE-5SM.

The second prototype, Type 118A, redesignated Type 120, first flew from Filton on 29 January 1932 and displayed the experimental marking 'R-6'. The aircraft unsuccessfully participated in the competition for Specification G.4/31, calling for a Wapiti and Gordon replacement. Purchased by the Air Ministry and serialled K3587, the aircraft performed lengthy trials with the A&AEE until it was struck off charge (SOC) on 21 January 1938.

## Production
Two aircraft were built; one Type 118 (No. 7561), registered G-ABEZ with experimental marking 'R-3' (K2873 during military trials) and one Type 118A (No. 7562), redesignated Type 120, displayed experimental marking 'R-6' (K3587 for military trials).

| Technical data – Type 118 and 120 | |
|---|---|
| ENGINE | (118) One 590hp Bristol Jupiter XFA; (120) one 650hp Pegasus I.M.3 |
| WINGSPAN | 40ft 8in |
| LENGTH | 34ft |
| HEIGHT | 12ft |
| WING AREA | 376sq ft |
| EMPTY WEIGHT | 3,632lb |
| ALL-UP WEIGHT | 5,200lb |
| MAX SPEED | (118) 165mph; (120) 175mph |
| CEILING | 25,600ft |

The Bristol Type 118 was registered as G-ABEZ in September 1930. During the aircraft's flight development in 1931 it displayed the experimental marking 'R-3'.

# Type 123 and 133

## Development
In late 1931, the Air Ministry issued Specification F.7/30 for a fighter armed with four machine guns and capable of at least 250mph. Bristol was one of six manufacturers to submit designs for eight aircraft, including the ultimate winner, the Gloster Gladiator.

## Design
Even though the Rolls-Royce Kestrel IV engine was favoured by the Air Ministry for the new fighter, the first of two designs proposed by Bristol, the Type 123, was powered by the Goshawk III. Destined to be the last biplane built by Bristol, the Type 123 was an impressive looking single-bay aircraft. It hosted many novel control features including full-span slots along the leading edge of the upper mainplane and the ailerons connected to 'interceptors' behind the outer slots, which rose up as the angle of attack increased.

The monoplane Mercury-powered Type 133 had a low cantilever wing incorporating an inverted gull wing shape. At the negative dihedral point was a retractable undercarriage and fabric-covered ailerons extended the full length of the outer wing section.

## Service
The Type 123 was first flown by Uwins on 12 June 1934, but the aircraft was seriously laterally unstable. The problem was caused by the inner slots venting, but even after these were clamped shut and the fin and rudder were increased in area, the problem remained. The Type 123's short life came to end soon after, partly because Uwins declared that any further development of the aircraft would be a waste of money.

Uwins was more impressed with the Type 133, which he first flew on 8 June 1934. In just 18 hours of flight testing, all performance and handling trials were completed and only spinning and diving tests were needed. These were carried out by Uwins on 8 March 1935 before delivery to Martlesham Heath when the aircraft was handed over to TW Campbell for a 30-minute handling flight. At 14,000ft, Campbell put the Type 133 into a right-hand spin, forgetting that he needed to raise the undercarriage. A flat spin immediately occurred and, after stalling the engine, Campbell was forced to take to his parachute at 8,000ft. After trapping his foot in the control column, he was unable to escape until the aircraft was down to 2,000ft. The aircraft crashed and burst into flames near Longwell Green, Bristol.

## Production
Two aircraft were built; one Type 123 biplane (No. 7775) and one Type 133 monoplane, 'R-10' (No. 7776).

## Type 123 and 133

| Technical data – Type 123 and 133 | |
|---|---|
| ENGINE | (118) One 695hp Rolls-Royce Goshawk III; one 640hp Bristol Mercury VIS.2 |
| WINGSPAN | (123) 29ft 7in; (133) 39ft |
| LENGTH | (123) 25ft 2in; (133) 28ft |
| HEIGHT | (123) 9ft 6in; (133) 9ft 9in |
| WING AREA | (123) 248sq ft; (133) 247sq ft |
| EMPTY WEIGHT | (123) 3,300lb; (133) 3,322lb |
| ALL-UP WEIGHT | (123) 4,737lb; (133) 7,738lb |
| MAX SPEED | (123) 235mph; (133) 260mph |

The Type 123 was the last Bristol biplane to be built at Filton, the Rolls-Royce Goshawk III-powered machine first flew in June 1934.

# Type 130 Bombay

## Development
The Bombay quietly served in the background while other aircraft types grabbed the headlines. It was designed for an unglamorous role, which it performed excellently in one of the world's harshest environments – the Middle East. Designed to Air Ministry Specification C.26/31, which called for a troop-carrier and bomber-transport, the Bombay was up against the Handley Page HP.51 (developed into the Harrow) and the Armstrong Whitworth AW.23, which would evolve into the excellent Whitley.

## Design
The largest aircraft to be designed at Filton to date, the Bombay would benefit from the indepth research information collected from the Bagshot and, as a result, it had a multi-spar wing of steel strip construction. A high-wing monoplane, the prototype Bombay (Type 130) was powered by a pair of 600hp Pegasus IIIM 3 engines with fixed-pitch propellers while production aircraft would have the improved 1,010hp Pegasus XXII with variable-pitch propellers. The prototype also differed by having spats around the main wheels.

Designed to be operated by a crew of three and capable of carrying 24 troops, the Bombay was fitted with two 0.303in Vickers 'K' machine-guns in power-operated turrets for self-defence and was also capable of carrying up to 2,000lb of bombs on external racks in an offensive role.

## Service
The prototype Bombay (known as the Type 130 until April 1937), K3583 first flew from Filton in the hands of Cyril Uwins on 23 June 1935 and, during the trials with the A&AEE, one of the test pilots was Flt Lt Arthur J 'Bill' Pegg who would later join Bristol, replacing Uwins in 1947 as chief test pilot. Because of the company's commitment to the Blenheim, all Bombay production was transferred to Short and Harland in Belfast, the first production aircraft, L5808 flew from Sydenham, southeast London, in March 1939.

The first Bombays in RAF service joined 216 Squadron at Heliopolis in October 1939 and operated alongside the vintage Valentia until the big biplanes were retired in November 1941. The Bombay was received by 117 Squadron, based in the Middle East at Khartoum, when it reformed in March 1941.

The only home unit to use the type in numbers from May 1940 through to February 1944 was 271 Squadron, based at Doncaster, Hendon and Errol. These aircraft supported hundreds of squadron movements throughout the country and delivered supplies to troops in France in June 1940.

In the Middle East, the Bombay carried out its dual role as a bomber, attacking targets along the North African coast, including the Libyan campaign in 1940, and also in Eritrea. Another Bombay achievement was to evacuate the Greek royal family from Crete to Egypt. As more modern transport types, such as the C-47/Dakota, began to take over the transport role, the Bombay fell by the wayside but remained in service in North Africa until August 1944.

## Production
One prototype, K3583 (No. 7809), and 50 production aircraft, serialled L5808 to L5857, were built by Short and Harland, Belfast to Contract No. 562468/36, all of which were delivered between April 1939 and June 1940.

## Type 130 Bombay

| Technical data – Bombay | |
|---|---|
| ENGINE | Two 1,010hp Bristol Pegasus XXII |
| WINGSPAN | 95ft 9in |
| LENGTH | 69ft 3in |
| HEIGHT | 19ft 6in |
| WING AREA | 1,340sq ft |
| EMPTY WEIGHT | 13,800lb |
| ALL-UP WEIGHT | 20,000lb |
| MAX SPEED | 192mph |
| CEILING | 25,000ft |
| RANGE | 2,230 miles |
| ACCOMMODATION | Three crew and 24 troops |

The first production Bombay, L5808 never entered operational service and only served with the A&AEE, Martlesham Heath. The aircraft crashed on take-off at Martlesham on 23 August 1939 after control was lost due to incorrect trimming.

Bombay L5857 of 216 Squadron operated from October 1939 until May 1943 when it was superseded by the Douglas Dakota. L5857 was destroyed in an air raid at Kufra on 25 September 1942.

The Type 130 prototype, K3583 was named *Josephine* and, after being withdrawn from flying duties in 1939, was used as a static airframe for development work.

## Type 130 Bombay

# Type 142

## Development

The Type 142, named 'Britain First', was designed for Lord Rothermere, the owner of the *Daily Mail*, and was a development of the Type 135, which never left the drawing board. Barnwell first sketched out the Type 135 in July 1933, confidently claiming that the aircraft, powered by a pair of Mercury engines, could reach 240mph. Rothermere wanted the aircraft built for his personal use so that he could claim that he owned the fastest commercial plane in Europe in response to aircraft developments in the USA. As a result, the Type 135 would evolve into the larger Type 143 with Aquila engines, while the smaller Type 142 would be powered by Mercury engines.

## Design

The Type 142 (No. 7838) was a low-wing stressed skin, light transport monoplane capable of carrying two crew and six passengers powered by a pair of Mercury VIS engines. A slim fuselage with a pointed half-glazed nose and retractable undercarriage helped the Type 142 break the 300mph barrier with ease. This was more than 50mph faster than the Gloster Gladiator, the winner of the F.7/30 competition.

## Service

First flown by Cyril Uwins from Filton on 12 April 1935, it had been registered as G-ADCZ in February. It was later donated by Lord Rothermere to the Air Council, given the experimental registration R-12 and delivered to the A&AEE at Martlesham Heath in June 1935 for trials. Allocated the serial K7557, the aircraft was used to investigate handling and served as a vehicle for trial installations until Blenheims became available.

The Type 142 was returned to Bristol on 12 July 1935 and then to the RAE on 30 April 1936. It was back at Bristol on 8 May 1936 and went on to serve with 24 and 101 squadrons during the remainder of that year, before returning to the A&AEE at the year end. It was transferred to the RAE again in April 1937 for directional stability and radio tests but, by 1940, the aircraft was relegated to ground duties and given the maintenance number 2211M. It was then moved to 10 SoTT (School of Technical Training) at Kirkham, Lancashire, on 10 September 1940 and remained there until it was scrapped in 1944 by Morris Motors.

| Technical data – Type 142 | |
|---|---|
| ENGINE | Two 650hp Bristol Mercury VIS 2 |
| WINGSPAN | 56ft 4in |
| LENGTH | 39ft 9in |
| HEIGHT | 12ft 10in |
| WING AREA | 469sq ft |
| EMPTY WEIGHT | 6,822lb |
| ALL-UP WEIGHT | 9,357lb |
| MAX SPEED | 307mph |
| RANGE | 1,000 miles |
| ACCOMMODATION | Two crew and four passengers |

## Type 142

The Bristol Type 142 being put through its paces by Cyril Uwins in 1935. (*The Aeroplane*)

The Type 142 presents a view of the massive drag-producing 'apron'-type wheel fairings that retracted neatly over the undercarriage, leaving only a small section of the tyre exposed. (*The Aeroplane*)

The pleasing lines of Type 142, K7557 are evident in this photograph, taken at Filton in autumn 1935. Crew and passenger comfort were not lacking and visibility for both was also good. The passengers enjoyed large windows in the side of the cabin and three 'skylights' along the spin. (*The Aeroplane*)

# Type 142

# Type 143

## Development
The Type 143, like its predecessor, shared its paper trail with the Type 135.

## Design
The Type 143 was a low-wing, enlarged, eight-passenger and two crew version of the Type 142 and was built alongside its more famous counterpart. The aircraft shared a large number (approximately 70 percent) of component parts. The main difference between the two was that the Type 143 was Aquila-powered with a sleeve-valve air-cooled radial engine, the fuselage was slightly bigger and the nose had a different profile to that of the Type 142.

## Service
The airframe was completed by early 1935 and was registered as G-ADEK on 22 March. Unfortunately, the Aquila engines were a long way from completing their trials and it was not until early 1936 that they were married to the airframe. On 20 January 1936, displaying the experimental serial R-14, the Type 143 first flew from Filton in the safe hands of Cyril Uwins. It almost sold to Imperial Airways in 1937, but Roy Fedden managed to secure the aircraft and it rarely ventured far from Filton. The aircraft remained at Filton as a flying test-bed for the Aquila engine, which came to nothing, as all development was abandoned by 1938. The Type 143 languished at Filton until 1940 when it was a scrapped.

Foreign interest was piqued by the Type 143, most significantly from Finland, and a military version of the aircraft with Mercury VI engines was seriously considered. Designated the Type 143F, it was clear that the aircraft could be easily adapted into a military version and a forward-firing 20mm Madsen cannon and a dorsal 'free' Lewis machine gun mounting was incorporated into the design. The Finnish government expressed interest and ordered nine Type 143Fs in February 1935 but, two months later, its attention was redirected to the Type 142.

| Technical data – Type 143 | |
|---|---|
| ENGINE | Two 500hp Bristol Aquila I |
| WINGSPAN | 56ft 4in |
| LENGTH | 43ft 2in |
| HEIGHT | 12ft 3in |
| WING AREA | 469sq ft |
| EMPTY WEIGHT | 7,000lb |
| ALL-UP WEIGHT | 11,000lb |
| MAX SPEED | 250mph |
| RANGE | 1,250 miles |
| ACCOMMODATION | Two crew and eight passengers |

The Type 143, just like the Type 142, never displayed its civilian registration but always bore its experimental marking 'R-14'.

Type 143 G-ADEK running up its Aquila engines at Filton in 1936. Note the 'ground crew' with a small extinguisher in his pocket and the clues behind as to the rapid expansion of Filton's facilities. (*The Aeroplane*)

Cyril Uwins taxies the Type 143 past visitors at the Bristol and Wessex Aeroplane Club's Garden Party at Whitchurch on 5 September 1936.

# Type 138 High Altitude Monoplane

## Development
As early as November 1933, Frank Barnwell had proposed a single-seat, high-altitude aircraft, powered by a two-stage supercharged Pegasus engine for research purposes. Not long after, the Air Ministry issued Specification 2/34 and after some minor modifications of Barnwell's original design, the Bristol Type 138A was born.

## Design
The Type 138A was a low-wing monoplane made of wood to keep the weight down to a minimum. A simple fixed undercarriage was also fitted for the same reason. The pilot, who would have to wear a specially developed pressure flying suit and oxygen-pressure helmet, accessed the cockpit via a plastic canopy. As well as suitably equipping the pilot, the engine needed to be modified to reach high altitude. This work was carried out by Clifford Tinson, who designed a two-stage compressor system; the first part being permanently engaged and the second being selected at altitude. The Type 138A's high aspect ratio, 66ft-span wing made the aircraft the largest single-seat monoplane in the world at the time.

## Service
The first aircraft, K4879, was first flown by Cyril Uwins on 11 May 1936; the flight was carried out with a standard Pegasus IV engine and a three-blade propeller. After completion of manufacturer's trials, the oxygen equipment was installed by the RAE and, on 15 August, the aircraft returned to Filton for fitment of a Pegasus PE VIS engine and a four-blade propeller.

The scene was set for the first attempt on the World Altitude Record, which took place from Farnborough on 28 September 1936. The pilot, Sqn Ldr FRD Swain, climbed to 49,967ft to gain the record for Britain, which was previously held at 48,698ft by France. In the meantime, the record was claimed by Italy in May 1937, raising the bar to 51,362ft.

To regain the record, K4879 was lightened with smaller main wheels and removal of the brakes and a finer pitch propeller was installed. The Pegasus engine was thoroughly overhauled and reconditioned for a second attempt on 3 June 1937. This time, the pilot, Flt Lt MJ Adam, took the aircraft to 53,937ft in a flight lasting 2 hours 1 5minutes. The record remained British until 22 October 1938, when Lt Col Mario Pezzi flew his Caproni to 56,850ft.

## Production
Two aircraft were built, one Type 138A serialled K4879 (No. 7840) and one two-seat Type 138B serialled L7037 (No. 8136). The latter aircraft was delivered to the RAE but no engine was ever installed. L7037 was relegated to instructional airframe duties on 9 September 1940 and allocated the number 2339M.

| Technical data – Type 138A High Altitude Monoplane | |
|---|---|
| ENGINE | One 460hp Bristol Pegasus PE VIS with two-stage supercharger |
| WINGSPAN | 66ft |
| LENGTH | 44ft |
| HEIGHT | 10ft 3in |
| WING AREA | 568sq ft |
| EMPTY WEIGHT | 4,391lb |
| ALL-UP WEIGHT | 5,340lb |
| MAX SPEED | 177mph at 45,000ft; 123mph at sea level |
| RATE OF CLIMB | 10,000ft in 11mins; 50,000ft in 62mins |

Bristol Type 138A, K4879 at Farnborough in September 1936, fully furnished for its attempt on the World Altitude Record for heavier-than-air aircraft.

# Type 146 and 148

## Development
In 1934, the Air Ministry issued Specification F.5/34 for an eight-gun fighter and, as a result, Bristol received a contract for a single prototype at a price of £11,500. However, rather than pin all company hopes on one prototype as it did with the Type 133, which was lost before it could be trialled, the company decided to make provision for a second prototype.

## Design
The new aircraft was designated the Type 146 and was a low-wing cantilever monoplane of similar proportions to the Type 133. The fuselage was a monocoque and the cockpit was enclosed by a one-piece sliding hood; the pilot was protected by a substantial crash-pylon should the aircraft overturn. The wing was made up of a straight centre section with outer sections that had a slight dihedral, all made of stress skin aluminium, although the ailerons were fabric covered. The Type 146 was armed with a quartet of 0.303in Browning machine guns mounted in each outer wing outside of the arc of the propeller.

After the Type 146 was ordered, the Air Ministry issued Specification A.39/34 for a new army co-operation monoplane to replace the Hawker Audax and Hector. Designated the Type 148, the aircraft shared many of the Type 146's components and featured the same monocoque construction. A two-seater, the crew were positioned in tandem under a long sliding canopy. The rear gunner/observer had a BV pillar mounting for a single 0.303in Lewis machine gun and a prone bombing position was placed in the floor. A pair of forward-firing 0.303in Brownings were mounted outside the propeller arc and bomb racks could also be fitted.

## Service
Powered by a Mercury IX, rather than the intended Perseus, the prototype Type 146, K5119, was first flown by Uwins on 11 February 1938. The aircraft went on to perform well in F.5/34 test at Martlesham Heath in April but, by then, the Air Ministry rightly thought that the future of the fighter aircraft lay with the water-cooled Rolls-Royce Merlin engine. The second prototype was cancelled and K5119 only survived until late May when the machine was damaged at Filton during an Empire Air Day.

The first Type 148, K6551 powered by a Mercury IX, first flew on 15 October 1937. Competing with the Westland Lysander in the A.39/34 trial, the Type 148 was let down by its low-wing and the Lizzie's (as the Lysander was known) fixed undercarriage sealed it for the Yeovil-built machine. The second Type 148 fitted with a Taurus II engine, designated Type 148B, K6552 first flew in May 1938. Both Type 148s were then used for test and evaluation for the remainder of their flying careers.

## Production
Three aircraft were built; one Type 146, K5119 (No. 7841); one Type 148s, K6551 (No. 7843); and one Type 148B, K6552 (No. 7844).

## Type 146 and 148

| Technical data – Type 146, 148 and 148B | |
|---|---|
| ENGINE | (146) One 840hp Bristol Mercury IX; (148) one 840hp Mercury IX or 905hp Perseus XII; (148B) one 1,050hp Taurus II |
| WINGSPAN | (146) 39ft; (148) 40ft |
| LENGTH | (146) 27ft; (148) 31ft; (148B) 31ft 4in |
| HEIGHT | (146) 10ft 4in; (148) 10ft 6in |
| WING AREA | (146) 220sq ft; (148) 275sq ft |
| EMPTY WEIGHT | (146) 3,283lb; (148) 4,450lb |
| ALL-UP WEIGHT | (146) 4,600lb; (148) 5,250lb |
| MAX SPEED | (146) 287mph; (148) 255mph; (148B) 290mph |
| CEILING | (146) 38,100ft; (148) 31,200ft |

The Mercury-powered Bristol Type 148, K6551 was the last single-engined piston aircraft built by Filton, disregarding the post-war Sycamore helicopter.

# Blenheim Mk I, IF, II and Bolingbroke I

## Design
Originally proposed in July 1935, the Type 142M (M for military), was the bomber version of the original *Britain First*. The main difference in this design was the wing, which was moved from its low position to the mid-fuselage releasing sufficient room for a bomb bay below. Behind the trailing edge of the wing, space was made for a dorsal turret and the nose compartment was redesigned to accommodate a bomb aimer. The new wing position also saw the tailplane raised by eight inches. All these modifications, including a host of internal changes pertinent to a military aircraft, were installed under a new Air Ministry Specification B28/35, which was drawn up in August 1935. By September, 150 Blenheim Mk Is were ordered direct from the drawing board. The first production machine, which was effectively the prototype, K7033, made its maiden flight from Filton on 25 June 1936. After service trials at Martlesham Heath, the design was officially given permission to proceed and production of the order began in December 1936. The third aircraft off the line, K7035, was the first Blenheim to be delivered to the RAF on 1 March 1937. The customer was 114 Squadron at Wyton, Cambridgeshire, and this first aircraft was, appropriately, a dual-controlled trainer, which would prove invaluable in training new pilots on the complex systems and higher performance range that the Blenheim introduced.

## Service
First envisaged as a long-range day fighter, the Mk IF was also capable of ground attack and bomber escort. This role was introduced in late 1938 and, by July 1939, the arrival of fighters such as the Bf109 saw the Blenheim lose its original speed advantage. Therefore, the Mk IF found itself in the night-fighting role, which when combined with the Airborne Interception (AI) radar, saw success.

The main difference between the Mk IF and the Mk I was the introduction of a gun tray below the fuselage, which was fitted with four Browning machine guns. Approximately 200 Mk Is were converted to Mk IFs, the first of which entered service with 25 Squadron at Hawkinge in December 1938. At the beginning of World War Two, 111 were in service with Fighter Command and one unit, 219 Squadron, was still operating in daylight at the height of the Battle of Britain. Mk IFs also served with Coastal Command, flying shipping protection duties, but, with the arrival of the Beaufighter Mk IF, the Blenheim fighter was rapidly being replaced by late 1940.

One Mk II, L1222, was converted from a Mk I, with long-range wing tanks, strengthened undercarriage and external bombs; fitted with Mercury VIII engines. Only one 'official' Blenheim PR Mk I was converted and used by 2 Camouflage Unit at Heston.

## Production
Blenheim Mk I production in Britain comprised 684 built at Filton; 250 by Avro at Chadderton; 250 by Rootes Securities at Speke, Liverpool and Blythe Bridge, Staffordshire. Overseas, 18 Mk I, were built by Fairchild Aircraft, Canada; 45 by Valtion Lentokonetehdas, Finland, and 16 by Ikarus AD in the former Yugoslavia.

| Technical data – Blenheim I, IF, II and Bolingbroke I | |
|---|---|
| ENGINE | Two 840hp Bristol Mercury VIII |
| WINGSPAN | 56ft 4in |
| LENGTH | (I) 39ft 9in; (Bolingbroke I) 42ft 9in |
| HEIGHT | 12ft 10in |
| WING AREA | 469sq ft |
| EMPTY WEIGHT | (I) 8,100lb; (Bolingbroke I) 9,800lb |
| ALL-UP WEIGHT | (I) 12,250lb; (Bolingbroke I) 12,500–14,400lb |
| MAX SPEED | (I) 285mph; (Bolingbroke I) 260–295mph |
| CEILING | (I) 32,000ft; (Bolingbroke I) 31,500ft |
| RANGE | (I) 1,125 miles; (Bolingbroke I) 1,950 miles |

**Blenheim Mk I L1295 pitches up for the camera prior to being delivered to 107 Squadron. The aircraft went on to serve with many second-line units. The Blenheim's career ended at Harlaxton, south Lincolnshire, with 12 PAFU (Pilots Advanced Flying Unit) in July 1943.**

Three Blenheim Mk Is captured just days before being delivered to the RAF's first Blenheim unit, 114 Squadron, in early March 1937.

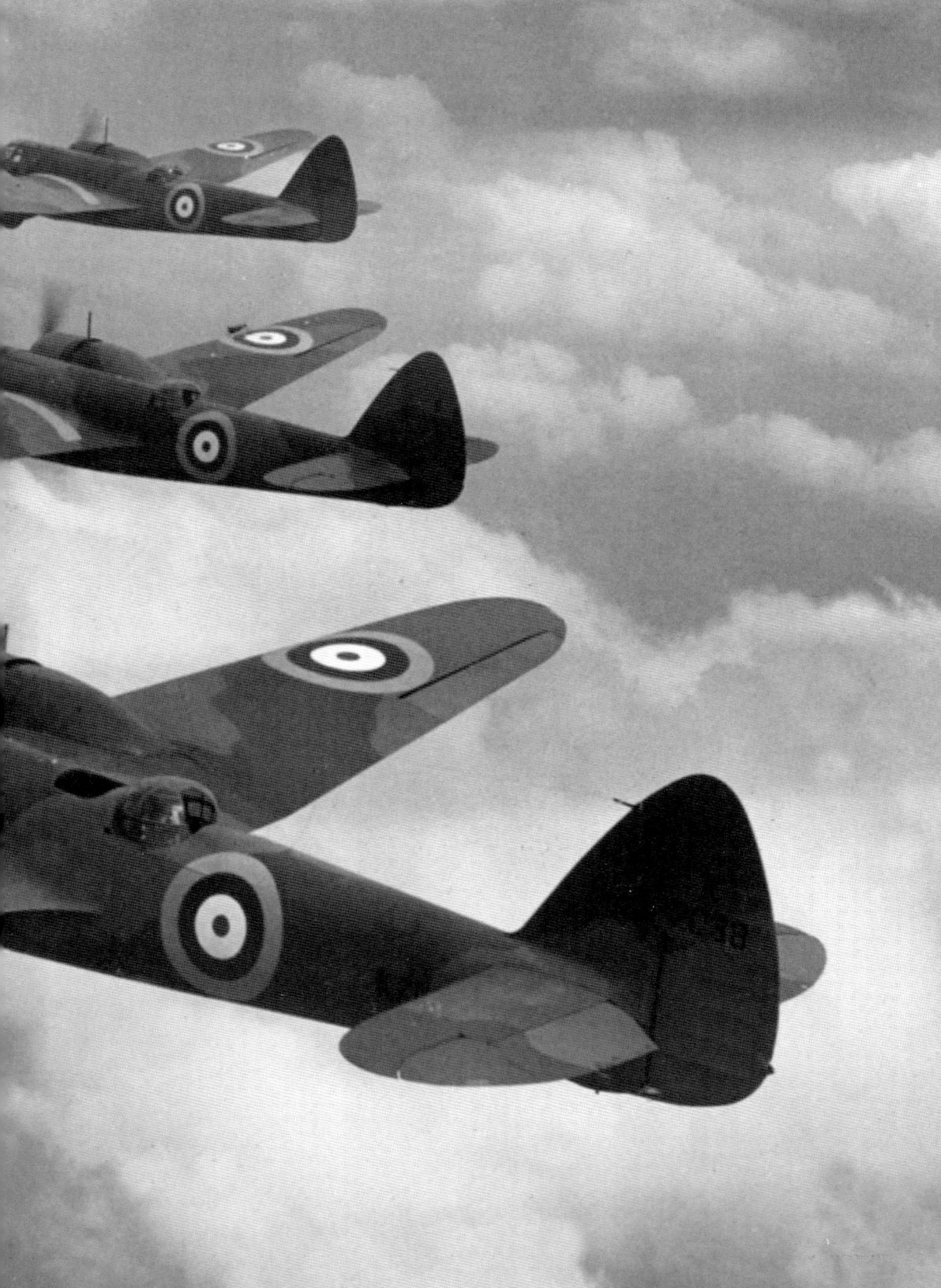

# Blenheim IV, IVF and Bolingbroke IV

## Design and service

Originally known as the Bolingbroke, a name later adopted by all Canadian-built machines, the long-nosed version of the Blenheim had its roots in Air Ministry Specification 11/36. The lengthened nose gave the navigator a new, and more roomy station by moving his position from behind the pilot to in front. The prototype, K7072, referred to as the Bolingbroke Mk I retained the same contour as the Blenheim Mk I but was extended forward. First flown on 24 September 1937, it was obvious from an early stage that the pilot's windscreen was too far away from his eyes and that the reflections caused by the multiple glazed panels caused problems. Over the coming months, attempts were made to rectify the issue until the familiar asymmetric glazed nose, with the navigator's position scalloped down to give the pilot a good line of sight, was tested at Martlesham Heath and approved for production from July 1938.

With production of the Blenheim Mk I already in full swing, a large number of the first Mk IVs were retrospectively converted before leaving the factory. It was not until January 1939 that the first Mk IVs entered RAF service with 53 Squadron at Odiham, Hampshire, for night reconnaissance duties. The first light bombers arrived on 90 Squadron at Bicester two months later and, by the beginning of the war, seven squadrons in 2 Group had been equipped with the Mk IV. The types bore the brunt of RAF Bomber Command's early operations and were in action from the first day of war until late 1943 in the Far East.

Like the Blenheim Mk IF before it, Mk IVF was converted in the same way, with the most obvious difference being the attachment of a four-gun under-fuselage gun pack. Approximately 125 Blenheims were converted to Mk IVFs and, initially, the type's main role was to serve with several Coastal Command fighter/reconnaissance squadrons on convoy patrol and protection duties. The big fighter entered service with 235, 236, 248 and 254 squadrons from April 1940 and, only days later, the first success was achieved. On 25 April, Plt Off Illingworth in R3628 of 254 Squadron at Hatston, Orkney, managed to shoot down an He 111 while escorting Royal Navy warships off Norway. Several Mk IVFs helped to cover the Dunkirk evacuation but only had a small role to play during the Battle of Britain, with only the odd skirmish recorded.

A handful of Mk IVFs were delivered to some Fighter Command night fighter squadrons in the summer of 1940, the first of which was 25 Squadron. The mark also saw some service in the Middle East and the Near East.

## Production

In total, 3,296 Blenheim Mk IVs were built, serving with 43 squadrons from UK airfields, they also operated in Aden, Burma, Ceylon, Egypt, Greece, India, Iraq, Java, Jordan, Malta, Palestine, Sudan, Sumatra Crete and Libya.

| Technical data – Blenheim and Bolingbroke IV | |
|---|---|
| ENGINE | Two 920hp Bristol Mercury XV |
| WINGSPAN | 56ft 4in |
| LENGTH | 42ft 9in |
| HEIGHT | 12ft 10in |
| WING AREA | 469sq ft |
| EMPTY WEIGHT | 9,800lb |
| ALL-UP WEIGHT | 12,500–14,400lb |
| MAX SPEED | 260–295mph |
| CEILING | 31,500ft |
| RANGE | 1,950 miles |
| ARMAMENT | One 0.303in machine gun in the port wing and two 0.303in Browning machine guns in a dorsal turret. Some aircraft were fitted with twin remotely-controlled, rearward-firing twin 0.303 Browning machine guns under the nose. Up to 1,320lb of bombs. |

*Above left*: Blenheim Mk IV, V6083, which started its career with 86 Squadron.

*Above right*: 53 Squadron at Odiham, Hampshire re-equipped with the Blenheim Mk IV, from the Hawker Hector in January 1939. The unit suffered heavy losses during the Battle of France in May 1940 and retained the Mk IV until July/August 1941, when it was replaced by the Lockheed Hudson.

*Below left*: The most prolific of all Fairchild-built Bolingbrokes was the Mk IV-T. None were lost in action, and several survive today, or have provided donor parts to other aircraft.

*Below right*: A brand new Blenheim Mk IV, N6212 showing the mark's final configuration. The N6212's operational career was short as it was lost while serving with 110 Squadron on 28 September 1939.

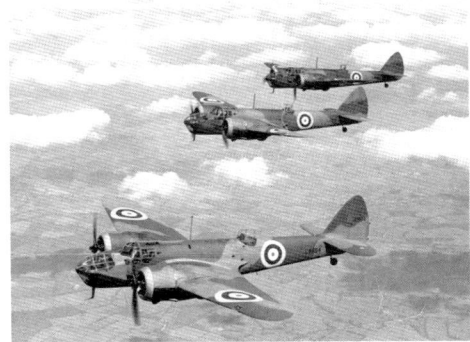

# Beaufort

## Development
It was originally the intention of the Air Ministry to re-equip Coastal Command's home-based squadrons with the Blackburn Botha while in the Far East; torpedo-bomber squadrons would be re-equipped with the Beaufort. However, the Botha proved unsuitable for the role and all Beauforts were transferred back to UK-based squadrons while in the Far East. It was the Australian-built Beauforts that stepped up to the plate, but not until October 1941.

## Design
The Beaufort was the result of combining two specifications, namely M.15/35 for a torpedo-bomber and G.24/35 for a general-purpose bomber. The general structure of the Beaufort was the same as the Blenheim although the torpedo-bomber was larger than its older sibling; the structural weight was lower because of several design refinements.

The development of the Beaufort concentrated on the engines and the armament. The Mk I was fitted with the Taurus VI, while the Mk IA was powered by the Taurus XII. New to the aircraft was Daimler-designed rear turret. The Mk II differed again by having a pair of Twin Wasp engines driving full-feathering propellers.

The Australian variants began with the Twin Wasp-powered Mk V, Va, VI, VII and VIII, the latter, ASV-radar equipped type being the most prolific with 520 built. A light transport conversion of various RAAF marks resulted in the Mk IX.

## Service
The prototype Beaufort, L4441, first flew on 15 October 1938, but the type did not enter service until November 1939 with 22 Squadron at Thorney Island, West Sussex, because of problems with the Taurus engines. That squadron's aircraft did not go into action until 15 April 1940 but made a good initial impression when it dropped the RAF's first 2,000lb bombs during a raid on enemy shipping off Norderney on 7 May 1940. RAF Beauforts often spent more time dropping bombs conventionally rather than delivering torpedoes, although they would become famous for attacking German warships such as the *Scharnhorst*, *Gneisenau*, *Prinz Eugen* and the *Lützow*, the latter being seriously damaged on 13 June 1941 by 42 Squadron.

The Australian-built Beauforts entered RAAF service in the summer of 1942 and served extensively across the Pacific theatre until the end of World War Two.

## Production
In total, 1,180 Beauforts were built at Filton and Banwell comprising, 1,103 Mk Is. 167 Mk II, and a single Mk IV prototype. Moreover, 121 Mk IIs were converted to T Mk II trainers with the rear turret faired over. Australian production totalled 700 aircraft made up of 50 Mk Vs, 30 Mk Vas, 40 Mk VIs, 60 Mk VIIs and 520 Mk VIIIs. Forty-six RAAF Beauforts of varying marks were converted to Mk IX light transports.

| Technical data – Beaufort I, II, V–VIII and IX | |
|---|---|
| ENGINE | (I) Two 1,130hp Bristol Taurus VI, XII or XVI; (II, V, VA, VIII and IX) two 1,200hp Pratt and Whitney Twin Wasp S3C4G; (Mk IV and VII) two 1,200hp Twin Wasp S1C3G; (IV) two 1,250hp Taurus XX |
| WINGSPAN | 57ft 10in |
| LENGTH | 44ft 3in |
| HEIGHT | 14ft 3in |
| WING AREA | 503sq ft |
| EMPTY WEIGHT | (I) 13,100lb; (II, V–VIII) 14,070lb; (IX) 13,000lb |
| ALL-UP WEIGHT | (I) 21,230lb; (II, V–VIII) 22,500lb; (IX) 20,000lb |
| MAX SPEED | (I) 260mph; (II, V–VIII) 265mph; (IX) 250mph |
| CEILING | (I) 16,500ft; (II, V–VIII) 22,500ft; (IX) 23,000ft |
| RANGE | (I) 1,600 miles; (II, V–VIII) 1,450 miles; (IX) 1,500 miles |

*Above left*: Beaufort Mk I, L9878, of 217 Squadron based at St Eval, Cornwall, in late 1940.

*Above right*: The Beaufort Mk II first entered service in Britain in October 1941 with 217 Squadron based at Thorney Island, West Sussex and St Eval, Cornwall. With much improved performance over the Mk I thanks to Twin Wasp engines, the Mk II had a Bristol Type 1 engine, Mk V rear turret, ASV radar and Yagi aerials.

*Right*: A crew in high spirits is kitted up before embarking across the North Sea to attack the battleship, *Prinz Eugen*.

# Beaufighter Mk IF and IC

## Development
As the dust began to settle following the Munich Crisis in 1938, the RAF suddenly realised that it had a distinct lack of modern fighters, especially heavily armed ones that could be employed as long-range escort or night fighters. As the Beaufort approached completion, it was suggested that the design team, led by Roy Fedden and Leslie Frise, could incorporate the major assemblies of the torpedo-bomber into a new design, designated the Type 156, and later named the Beaufighter. A draft proposal for the new aircraft was produced in a few days and submitted to the Air Ministry in October 1938. On 17 July 1939, an order for four prototypes was placed to Specification F.17/39 and was followed by a production order for 300 aircraft.

## Design
The Beaufighter was a mid-wing cantilever monoplane of all-metal construction with a conventional fuselage and tail unit structures, complete with a retractable main and tail undercarriage. Power for the four prototypes was provided by several different marks of Hercules sleeve-valve, while the production Mk IF settled for a pair of 1,400hp Hercules XIs. The standard armament of the Mk IF was four 20mm cannon in the nose, four 0.303in in the starboard wing and two more machine guns in the leading edge of the port wing. An AI Mk IV was installed in the nose.

The Mk IC was a dedicated Coastal Command variant furnished with an additional radio and navigational equipment.

## Service
The first prototype, R2052, flew on 17 July 1939, while the remainder were in the air by May 1940. The Beaufighter Mk IF first entered RAF service with the Fighter Interception Unit (FIU) at Tangmere, West Sussex, on 12 August 1940. The FIU machines flew its first operational sortie on 4/5 September; the same month, the type joined 25, 29, 219 and 604 squadrons at North Weald, Essex, Digby, Lincolnshire, Redhill, Surrey and Middle Wallop, Hampshire. The first night victory using the AI radar was achieved by 604 Squadron on 19 November when a Ju 88 was shot down over Oxfordshire.

The Coastal Command Mk IF first joined 252 Squadron at Chivenor in December 1940, replacing the Blenheim IVF in the same role. The dedicated Mk IC variant began arriving from March 1941.

By late 1940, healthy production meant that the Beaufighter was also despatched to the Middle East as a long-range day fighter flown by 252 and 272 Squadrons. The range was extended by fitting 50-gal internal fuel tanks to the fuselage floor, although this method was updated with extra tanks in the outer wings and this resulted in a reduction in machine guns.

## Production
Beaufighter Mk IF and Mk IC production totalled 910 aircraft and was carried out at Filton and Whitchurch by Bristol, by Fairey at Stockport and at the Ministry of Aircraft Production (MAP) Shadow Factory at Old Mixon, Weston-super-Mare.

| Technical data – Beaufighter I | |
|---|---|
| ENGINE | Two 1,400hp Bristol Hercules III, X or XI |
| WINGSPAN | 57ft 10in |
| LENGTH | 41ft 4in |
| HEIGHT | 15ft 10in |
| WING AREA | 503sq ft |
| EMPTY WEIGHT | 13,800lb |
| ALL-UP WEIGHT | 21,000lb |
| MAX SPEED | 330mph |
| CEILING | 29,000ft |
| RANGE | 1,500 miles (1,750 miles with extra wing tanks) |

*Above*: The prototype Bristol Type 156 Beaufighter without armament at Filton in July 1939.

*Below left*: X7543 was one of 239 Beaufighter Mk IFs built by Bristol at Weston-super-Mare and delivered between February 1941 and February 1942. X7543 was retained by Bristol for trials and continued flying until April 1944.

*Below right*: The first Weston-super-Mare-built Mk IF was X7540, which was delivered to the RAF in February 1941 and is pictured after arriving at the A&AEE, Boscombe Down, Wiltshire, a few days later.

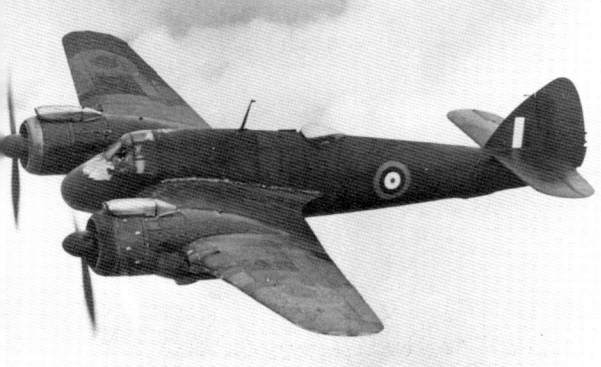

# Beaufighter Mk II, IIF and V

## Development
By 1940, the demand for the Bristol Hercules engines had reached a point where it became prudent to begin experiments with an alternative powerplant. Priority was being given to the Hercules-powered Short Stirling and another alternative, the Rolls-Royce Griffon, had already been allocated to Fairey Firefly production. This still left the Merlin, which was in good supply by late 1940, despite the demands placed upon its production.

## Design
Three Beaufighter Mk Is, R2058, R2061 and R2062 were selected for Mk II conversion with a pair of Merlin XX engines. However, the Merlin XX was not available at first and, after being delivered to Hucknall, R2058 was fitted with a pair of 1,075hp Merlin X engines instead. In this form, the aircraft first flew in July 1940 and demonstrated a slight improvement in performance but also displayed directional stability issues because of a slightly altered centre of gravity. Despite this, the Mk II was cleared for RAF service and the stability problem was only retrospectively solved with a 12-degree dihedral tailplane. A tendency to swing on take-off was additionally helped by a dorsal fin extension; both of these modifications were applied to all subsequent marks of Beaufighter. The dorsal fin extension and dihedral tailplane were first trialled on Mk IIF, T3032. Rotol airscrews with wooden, non-feathering Schwartz blades were made as standard for all service Mk IIFs.

One other Merlin-powered variant was the Mk V of which only two aircraft, R2274 and R2306, were converted. These were fitted with an experimental Boulton-Paul power-operated, four-gun turret mounted directly behind the cockpit. Both aircraft were trialled by 406 and 600 squadrons, but the idea was not pursued.

## Service
The first production Mk IIF, powered by Merlin XX engines, was first flown on 22 March 1941 and was in service by April, initially with 600 Squadron, at Colerne, Wiltshire. The Mk IIF re-equipped eight home-defence night-fighter squadrons out of a total of 15 operational units with which it served. The Mk IIF also served with 721, 723, 726, 733, 762, 775, 779, 781, 788, 789, 797 and 798 squadrons of the Fleet Air Arm.

## Production
Three Beaufighter Mk II prototypes, followed by 447 production Mk IIF serialled R2270–2479, T3009–3447 and V8131–8218, were delivered between March 1941 and July 1942, all built at Filton. R2274 and R2306 were converted on the production line at Filton to Mk V standard.

# Beaufighter Mk II, IIF and V

| Technical data – Beaufighter II, IIF and V | |
|---|---|
| ENGINE | Two 1,250hp Rolls-Royce Merlin XX |
| WINGSPAN | 57ft 10in |
| LENGTH | 42ft 9in |
| HEIGHT | 15ft 10in |
| WING AREA | 503sq ft |
| EMPTY WEIGHT | 13,800lb |
| ALL-UP WEIGHT | 21,000lb |
| MAX SPEED | 330mph |
| CEILING | 29,000ft |
| RANGE | 1,500 miles (1,750 miles with extra wing tanks) |

*Above left*: The prototype Beaufighter Mk II, R2058 having its Rolls-Royce Merlin X engines run-up at Hucknall, Nottinghamshire, prior to its maiden flight in July 1940.

*Above right*: The first production Beaufighter Mk IIF, R2270 was completed in March 1941. After flight trials with the A&AEE and the RAE, the aircraft served operationally with 604 and 406 Squadrons before being struck off charge (SOC) in February 1944.

*Below*: The first of two Mk IIs, converted to Mk V standard with a Boulton Paul turret mounted behind the pilot's cockpit. Installed to improve the aircraft's field of fire, the cumbersome turret reduced the performance of the Beaufighter and the idea was abandoned.

# Bisley Mk I and Blenheim V

## Development
Originally known as the Bisley Mk I but later renamed the Blenheim Mk V, this variant was an attempt to rectify the many shortcomings of the previous marks. Unfortunately, the Mk V was nothing more than a disappointment and was very unpopular both with the crews who had to fly it and the mechanics who had to keep it flying.

## Design
The Mk V story began in 1940 when a redesign of the Blenheim was called for under Air Ministry Specification B.6/40. Prior to this, Operational Requirements Nos. 83 and 84 had also called for an improvement in the aircraft's ground attack capability and it was to these specifications that Bristol set to work trying to improve the Blenheim.

The first major alteration was to the power plants, which were uprated to a pair of Mercury 30s. Their increased horsepower was cancelled out by the 600lb of increased armour protection for the crew, a modified oxygen system and heavier BX turret, which made the average loaded weight another 2,000lb heavier than the Mk IV.

Two versions were built at the prototype stage, the first Type 160 Bisley Mk I, AD657, flew from Filton on 24 February 1941. This aircraft was a two-seat close-support aircraft with a solid nose containing four 0.303in machine guns. The second prototype, AD661 was designed as a three-seat high-altitude day bomber with a new semi-glazed nose, and due to its lack of symmetry was referred to as a 'duck bill'. The Type 160 evolved into the Type 160BS, which by then had been designated as the Blenheim Mk VB. The latter was not built in great numbers and the major production version was the Type 160D (Mk VD), a tropicalized version of the Blenheim Mk VA.

## Service
The Blenheim Mk Vs tentatively entered service with 139 Squadron in June 1942 but were replaced by Mosquitoes before becoming operational. By late 1942, the type was serving with 13, 18, 114 and 614 squadrons in North Africa, but poor performance and heavy losses saw them all replaced by American-built Baltimores and Bostons. The Mk V also saw service in the Far East including Burma and Ceylon and a few also served with 8 Squadron in the Persian Gulf. The last Mk V operations were flown by 244 Squadron in Oman before being replaced by Wellington XIIIs in April 1944.

## Production
In total, 942 Blenheim Mk Vs were built, only two of them (AD657 and AD661), the prototypes, were built at Filton, while the remainder were built by Rootes Securities Ltd at Blythe Bridge, Staffordshire. The last was delivered in June 1943.

| Technical data – Bisley Mk I and Blenheim Mk V | |
|---|---|
| ENGINE | (Bisley) Two 950hp Bristol Mercury XVI; (V) two 950hp Mercury 25 or 30 |
| WINGSPAN | 56ft 1in |
| LENGTH | (Bisley) 43ft 4in; (V) 43ft 11in |
| HEIGHT | 12ft 10in |
| WING AREA | 469sq ft |
| EMPTY WEIGHT | 11,000lb |
| ALL-UP WEIGHT | 17,000lb |
| MAX SPEED | (Bisley) 262mph; (V) 260mph |
| CEILING | 31,000ft |
| RANGE | 1,600 miles |

*Above left*: The first of two prototype Blenheim Mk Vs (built by Rootes), DJ702 was delivered to the A&AEE in late 1941. The aircraft later served with 12 PAFU (Pilots Advanced Flying Unit) and 17 SFTS (Service Flying Training School) until it came to grief at Cranwell, Lincolnshire, on 19 April 1945.

*Above right*: The first prototype Bisley Mk I (Blenheim Mk V), AD657 saw service with the A&AEE before being SOC on 13 July 1942.

*Below left*: A 614 (County of Glamorgan) Mk V being prepared for an operation at dawn from Canrobert, Algeria.

*Below right*: The 8 Squadron Mk V, BA612 was one of several that took part in attacks against Italian forces in East Africa. The unit operated the Mk V from September 1942 until January 1944.

# Beaufighter Mk VI, VIC and VIF

## Development
It was fortunate, for both Bristol and the RAF, that the envisaged shortage of Hercules engines did not materialise and that all focus reverted to the Beaufighter's original powerplant while the Merlin-powered machines were pushed to the back burner. In fact, production of the original engine began to rise and, in late 1941, the 1,650hp, Hercules VI was made available to the Beaufighter. The resulting variant was the Mk VI and, like the Mk I before it, it was produced for both Fighter Command (Mk VIF) and Coastal Command (Mk VIC) in some quantity.

## Design
Three aircraft were used to trial the new Hercules VI and XVI engine, both being accepted as the standard powerplants for the Beaufighter Mk VI. The extra power generated by the engine gave the Beaufighter more flexibility with equipment and weapons. Machine guns in the wings could be replaced by a 50-gallon tank on the starboard side and a 24-gallon tank on the port to give a potential range of 1,750 miles. A pair of 250lb bombs could be carried under the wings, or eight 90lb rocket projectiles. Following trials, which began in March 1942, the Beaufighter was also found to be more than capable of carrying a single American or British-built standard marine torpedo. Nicknamed the 'Torbeau', the combination would prove to be lethal against enemy shipping.

## Service
The Mk VIF first entered service with 255 Squadron at High Ercall in March, going on to equip a total of four home-based night-fighter units; the type remained in service with 68 Squadron at Castle Camps until July 1944. The Mk VIC with its rocket and torpedo carrying capability was initially known as the Mk VIC (ITF) (Interim Torpedo Fighter) until the arrival of the specialist Mk X. The ITFs helped form the first Beaufighter Strike Wing at North Coates, Lincolnshire, in November 1942 made up of 143 Squadron with fighter variants, 246 Squadron with bombs and 254 Squadron with 'Torbeaus'. The North Coates Strike Wing achieved its first successful attack against enemy shipping on 18 April 1943 and, from May 1943, Coastal Command's capability rose when the rocket-armed version of the Mk VIC also entered squadron service.

The Mk VIF also served in the Burma/India theatre with 176 Squadron, at first serving in the defence of Calcutta. This variant was served with four USAAF units (414th, 415th, 416th and 17th NFS (Night Fighter Squadron)) as part of the 1st Tactical Air Command in the Mediterranean theatre.

## Production
Total Beaufighter Mk VIF production was 1,842 (including one prototype) built at Filton and Whitchurch by Bristol and by Rootes Securities Ltd, Blythe Bridge, Staffordshire. The Mk VIC was built by Fairey at Stockport and at the MAP Shadow Factory at Old Mixon, Weston-super-Mare.

| Technical data – Beaufighter Mk VI, VIF and VIC | |
|---|---|
| ENGINE | Two 1,650hp Bristol Hercules VI or XVI |
| WINGSPAN | 57ft 10in |
| LENGTH | 41ft 4in |
| HEIGHT | 15ft 10in |
| WING AREA | 503sq ft |
| EMPTY WEIGHT | 14,900lb |
| ALL-UP WEIGHT | 21,000lb |
| MAX SPEED | 330mph |
| CEILING | 29,000ft |
| RANGE | 1,500 miles (1,750 miles with extra wing tanks) |

The first rocket projectile-armed Beaufighter was Mk VIC, EL329, pictured during its brief time at Boscombe Down. The aircraft was lost on 24 September 1942 following an engine failure and subsequent crash near Bulford Camp, Wiltshire.

Beaufighter Mk VIF KV912 of the 416th NFS (Night Fighter Squadron) based at Lecce, Italy, in late 1943. The aircraft has three nicknames; the aircraft as a whole is nicknamed 'Fluff' while the port Hercules is named 'Patsy' and starboard 'Amby'.

# Beaufighter Mk X

## Development
While the Mosquito and Beaufighter had been around since the early stages of World War Two, it was not until 1943 that they had both been fully developed into heavily armed machines capable of packing a punch sufficient to sink an enemy ship or submarine. The Mk X version of the Beaufighter was available in great numbers thanks to the Mosquito taking over the night-fighting role.

## Design
Powered by a pair of Bristol Hercules XVII radial engines, each developing 1,770hp, the Beaufighter was a formidable-looking aircraft. It was not as fast or as manoeuvrable as the Mosquito but it could pack the same punch with accuracy, thanks to its excellent stability. In the anti-shipping role, the Beaufighter could be fitted with RPs under each wing, up to 250lbs of bombs or a single 1,650lb or 2,127lb torpedo. Later production Beaufighter Mk Xs also had the added advantage of an ASV radar fitted in a modified 'thimble'-shaped nose, giving a greater operational capability. With a range of nearly 1,500 miles, its crew of two could operate the Beaufighter against any target along the Norwegian or Danish coasts.

Post-war, 35 Mk Xs were converted into target-towing TT Mk 10s and the final British-built Beaufighter variant was the Mk XIC, which was powered by Hercules XVII engines.

## Service
The Beaufighter Mk X first entered service with 248 Squadron at Predannack, Cornwall, in June 1943 and, by the end of the war, the mark had re-equipped 30 RAF squadrons. The Mk X quickly gained a well-deserved reputation as a formidable anti-shipping strike aircraft especially when it was operated as part of a strike wing. The Dallachy Strike Wing alone flew 2,230 sorties, sunk 15 ships and damaged 55 others during its brief existence. The 236 and 254 Squadrons of the North Coates Wing achieved fame when they located and destroyed five U-boats in the space of 48 hours in March 1945.

Post-war, the Mk X remained in the Coastal Command inventory until February 1950 when it was replaced by the Brigand. Another useful extension of the type's service came with the TT Mk 10 delivered between 1948 and 1950. It was a TT Mk 10, RD761, which marked the end of the Beaufighter in RAF service when it flew a final sortie from Seletar, Singapore, on 12 May 1960.

Beaufighter Mk X NE343 during rocket projectile and overload tank trials with the A&AEE in March 1944. The aircraft later served with 455 (RAAF) Squadron at Langham, Norfolk, and Dallachy, Moray, and was SOC in January 1947.

## Production

Beaufighter Mk X production totalled 2,205 aircraft built at the MAP Shadow Factory at Old Mixon, Weston-super-Mare, and by Rootes Securities Ltd, Blythe Bridge, Staffordshire. In total, 163 Mk VICs were built and 35 Mk Xs were converted to TT Mk 10.

| Technical data – Beaufighter Mk X | |
| --- | --- |
| ENGINE | Two 1,735hp Bristol Hercules XVII |
| WINGSPAN | 57ft 10in |
| LENGTH | 42ft 6in |
| HEIGHT | 15ft 10in |
| WING AREA | 503sq ft |
| EMPTY WEIGHT | 15,600lb |
| ALL-UP WEIGHT | 25,400lb |
| MAX SPEED | 330mph |
| CEILING | 29,000ft |
| RANGE | 1,500 miles (1,750 miles with extra wing tanks) |

*Right*: A quartet of Beaufighter Mk Xs of 404 (Buffalo) Squadron Royal Canadian Air Force, which served at Dallachy from October 1944 to April 1945.

*Below left*: 163 Hercules XVII-powered Beaufighter Mk XICs were built for Coastal Command in the serial ranges JL876 to JL948 and JM105 to JM267.

*Below right*: Beaufighter TT.10, RD788 of the Malta C&TTS (Communication & Target Towing Squadron) at Luqa, Malta, which operated the aircraft until 1958.

# Buckingham and Buckmaster

## Development
Completely overshadowed and surpassed in all respects by the de Havilland Mosquito, the Buckingham was originally planned back in 1940 as a replacement, to be ready by 1942, for the Blenheim in the tactical day-bomber role. It was developed too late for the role for which it was intended, although a training derivative, named the Buckmaster, did give the RAF ten years of post-war service.

## Design
The Buckingham was a development of a day-bomber project called the Beaumont, which was designed to Specification B.2/41 and intended to meet a separate requirement for a close support bomber. The Beaumont was to be fitted with a pair of Hercules engines, but when the more powerful Centaurus became available, all focus was on the Buckingham. This is where the Buckingham's problems began; the early 18-cylinder Centaurus engines suffered a host of teething troubles combined with an ever-changing role.

Built in two variants, the Buckingham B Mk 1 was capable of carrying up to 4,000lbs of bombs and was furnished with ten 0.303in machine-guns; four mounted in the nose, four in a dorsal turret and two at the rear of a ventral copula, which was occupied by a bomb-aimer/navigator. The Buckingham was the fastest turreted bomber to be built by a British aircraft manufacturer. The second variant was the C Mk 1, which was designed to be a high-speed courier transport capable of carrying four passengers and three crew. Fitted with higher capacity fuel tanks and the dorsal turret removed, the C Mk 1 had an impressive range of up to 3,000 miles.

First planned in 1943, the Buckmaster T Mk 1 featured dual-controls and side-by-side seating for an instructor and pupil. With a combined 5,000hp from its two Centaurus VII radials, the Buckmaster was one of the most powerful and fastest aircraft ever to serve the RAF in the training role.

## Service
The prototype Buckingham, DX249, first flew on 4 February 1943, but it was not until a year later that the first production machines began rolling off the Filton line. By this time, the original production order for 400 aircraft was reduced to 119 and with no role for the B Mk 1, the last 65 were built as C Mk 1s. The transport version carried out services to Malta and Egypt for the remainder of the war and early post-war period.

The first of two Buckmaster prototypes, TJ714, first flew on 27 October 1944 and, by 1945, the first production machines were already rolling off the line. The 110 aircraft built were extensively used by 6, 132, 228 and 238 OCUs, CFS, the Empire Central Flying School (ECFS) and 8, 36, 45, 84 and 154 squadrons from 1945 to 1956. The type proved to be an excellent introduction for aircrew converting to the Brigand light bomber, which would see action overseas.

## Production
Four prototypes (DX249, DX255, DX259 and DX266) and 119 production Buckinghams (Type 163s) were built; the latter was made up of 54 B Mk 1s and 65 C Mk 1s. Two prototypes (TJ714 and TJ717) and 110 (Type 166) were built.

| Technical data – Type 163 Buckingham and Type 166 Buckmaster | |
|---|---|
| ENGINE | (163) Two 2,400hp Bristol Centaurus IV, VII or XI; (166) Centaurus VII |
| WINGSPAN | 71ft 10in |
| LENGTH | 46ft 10in |
| HEIGHT | 17ft 7in |
| WING AREA | 708sq ft |
| EMPTY WEIGHT | (163) 24,040lb; (166) 23,000lb |
| ALL-UP WEIGHT | (163) 36,900lb; (166) 33,700lb |
| MAX SPEED | (163) 335mph; (166) 352mph |
| CEILING | (163) 25,000ft; (166) 30,000ft |
| RANGE | (163) 2,200 miles; (166) 2,000 miles |

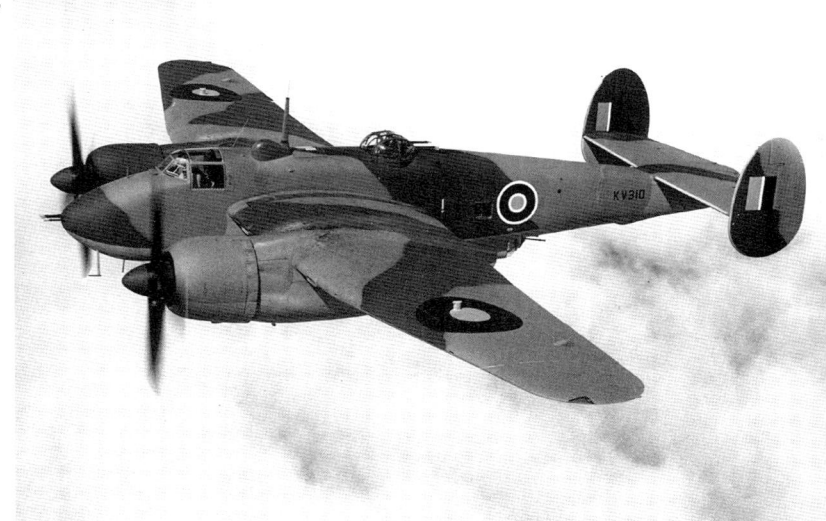

*Right*: Buckingham B Mk 1, KV310, during trials with the A&AEE at Boscombe Down in mid-1944. The aircraft was one of many Buckinghams SOC and declared scrap on 15 May 1947.

*Below left*: A total of 65 Buckinghams, serialled KV338 to KV479, were built as C Mk 1s, operating as high-speed, long-range courier aircraft. Their limited capacity of just four passengers made them very uneconomical to operate.

*Below right*: Buckmaster T Mk 1, RP185 of 228 OCU (Operational Conversion Unit) at Leeming, North Yorkshire, a unit tasked with training night fighter and all-weather fighter crews.

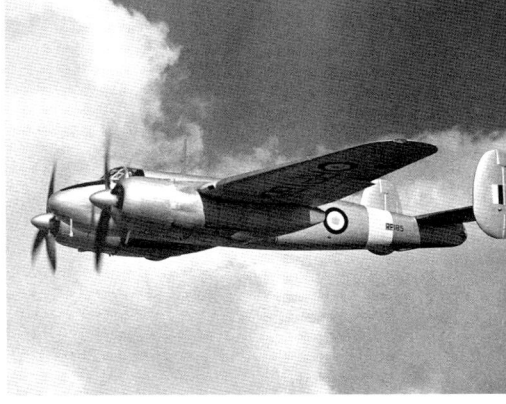

RP246, a Buckmaster T Mk 1, was the last of 100 built by Bristol at Filton and delivered to the RAF between March 1945 and April 1946. This aircraft is pictured in service with the Empire Central Flying School (ECFS) based at Hullavington, Wiltshire.

# Beaufighter Mk 21

## Development
The RAAF was first supplied with 50 Beaufighter Mk ICs and Mk VICs in 1941 and 1942, but by 1944, a licence had been agreed and Australia began to build its own machines with the designation Mk 21. Constructed by the Department of Aircraft Production (DAP), the Mk 21 would expand the reputation of the Beaufighter across the Far East and Pacific theatres of war.

## Design
Very similar in design to the Beaufighter Mk X, the Mk 21 was powered by a pair of Hercules CVII or CXVIII engines. Built as an attack/torpedo variant, the Mk 21 was armed with four 20mm cannon in the nose, four 0.5in Brownings in the wings, eight 5in HVAR, a pair of 250lb bombs and a single Mk 13 torpedo. Mk 21s also had the luxury feature of an autopilot, visible from the outside from a bulge on top of the nose.

Just like the RAF's Mk X, several Mk 21s were converted into target tugs; the first of them, A8-265, was modified on 8 July 1945.

## Service
The Beaufighter Mk 21 first entered RAAF service with 31 Squadron in September 1944, a seasoned unit formed in August 1942 with the Mk IC. In November 1944, 30 Squadron received its first Mk 21s, while 93 and 22 squadrons saw their first examples in January and February 1945, respectively.

It was during operations against the Japanese that the grim nickname 'Whispering Death' was applied to the Beaufighter while operating with the RAF and RAAF. The Mk 21 saw extensive action against the Japanese; 31 Squadron become adept at scoring air-to-air victories as well as destroying ground targets. 30 Squadron, serving as part of the Australian 1st TAF (Tactical Air Force), operated in the Netherlands East Indies (NEI) from November 1944, roaming over the Celebes Sea. The unit also supported Australian ground forces in Borneo and, in May 1945, 30 Squadron flew from Tarakan in support of the landings at Balikpapan, NEI.

22 Squadron first went into action in February 1945 when nine Beaufighter Mk 21s carried out an attack on Tandao in the Celebes Sea. The unit played an important role in Operation *Oboe Six* when the Australians invaded Tarakan, Indonesia.

93 Squadron began operations on 26 July 1945, which were concluded on 13 August when four aircraft flew an armed reconnaissance to Kuching airfield in Malaysia, and eight more attacked Tromboul airfield. Despite this lack of action, 93 Squadron had the honour of filming the Japanese surrender at RAAF Laverton, Singapore, on 25 September 1945.

## Production
In total, 365 Beaufighter Mk 21s, serialled A8–1 to A8–365, were built by the Beaufort Division, DAP, at Fisherman's Bend, Victoria, Australia.

| Technical data – Beaufighter Mk 21 | |
|---|---|
| ENGINE | Two 1,735hp Bristol Hercules XVIII |
| WINGSPAN | 57ft 10in |
| LENGTH | 41ft 4in |
| HEIGHT | 15ft 10in |
| WING AREA | 503sq ft |
| EMPTY WEIGHT | 15,600lb |
| ALL-UP WEIGHT | 25,400lb |
| MAX SPEED | 330mph |
| CEILING | 29,000ft |
| RANGE | 1,500 miles (1,750 miles with extra wing tanks) |

*Above left*: In total, 365 Beaufighter Mk 21s were built by the Department of Aircraft Production (DAP) at Fishermen's Bend, Melbourne, between May 1944 and November 1945. Note the bulge on the nose for the autopilot, which was one of the few unique features of the mark.

*Above right*: Beaufighter Mk 21, A8-229, during its service with 8 Communications Unit when it was employed to transport senior staff officers during the summer of 1945.

*Below left*: After being placed in storage in October 1945, A8-350 was later modified as a target tug in August 1950 and remained in service until 1956.

*Below right*: Early production (possibly the first aircraft, A8-1) Mk 21, christened *Red Cliffs*, presents the key features of the mark. It had 20mm cannon in the nose, four 0.5in Brownings in the wings, rails for eight 5in HVAR (High Velocity Aircraft Rocket), two racks for 250lb bombs and empty shackles for a single Mk 13 torpedo.

# Brigand

## Development

The Beaufighter would always be a tough act to follow, and this was complicated by the change of requirement from that of a torpedo-bomber/torpedo-fighter to one of a light bomber required by a post-war RAF, especially for those units that were serving in the Middle and Far East.

Originally named the Buccaneer, the Brigand was designed in response to Specification H.7/42, which was effectively a Beaufighter variant with a crew of three and with power provided by a pair of Hercules VIII engines. This idea was soon abandoned, and the aircraft instead drew heavily from its unsuccessful sibling, the Buckingham.

## Design

The Type 164 Brigand utilized the wings, tail assembly and twin Centaurus engines of the Buckingham combined with a redesigned fuselage with a much smaller cross-section. No power-operated turret was installed, and the cockpit was rebuilt to accommodate three crew under a large transparent canopy that could be jettisoned in the event of an emergency. The first 13 Brigands built were designated TF Mk 1, capable of carrying a single torpedo. The main production B Mk I variant featured extra armour plating, four 20mm cannon in the nose and provision for a single machine gun in the rear of the cockpit.

The Met Mk 3 was an unarmed weather reconnaissance variant while the T Mk 4 radar trainer, also unarmed, featured an AI Mk X radar in the nose and black-out blinds for the trainee's rear cockpit. The final version, which was converted from B Mk 1s and T Mk 4s, was the T Mk 5 radar trainer installed with an AI Mk 21 radar in a slightly longer nose.

## Service

Four Brigand prototypes were ordered in April 1943 the first of them, MX988, made its maiden flight on 4 December 1944. The early production TF Mk 1s served with the Air-Sea Weapons Development Unit at Gosport from May 1946, but this variant was destined never to join Coastal Command squadrons.

The B Mk 1 entered service with 84 Squadron at Habbaniya (modern-day Iraq), in June 1949 and 8 Squadron at Aden (modern day South Yemen), from October 1949. In the Far East, 45 Squadron began replacing its Beaufighters with the Met Mk 3 from May 1949 and the B Mk 1 from October. Joined at Tengah, Singapore, by 84 Squadron in April 1950, the two squadrons carried out many successful strikes as part of Operation Firedog against terrorists in Malaya. The Brigand B Mk 1 was not without its problems, and far more were lost in accidents due to mechanical failure than to enemy action. The RAF's last piston-engined attack aircraft was withdrawn from operations in February 1953.

The T Mk 4 first flew in 1949 and entered service with 228 OCU at Leeming in July 1951. It was joined by the T Mk 5 from 1955 and, by the time of their retirement in 1958, the two aircraft had training approximately 600 radar navigators.

## Production

In total, 147 Brigands were built, including four prototypes, 16 Met Mk 3s and nine T Mk 4s. Up to 30 B Mk 1s and T Mk 4s were converted to T Mk 5 standard.

| Technical data – Type 164 Brigand | |
|---|---|
| ENGINE | (163) Two 2,500hp Bristol Centaurus 57 |
| WINGSPAN | 72ft 4in |
| LENGTH | 46ft 5in |
| HEIGHT | 17ft 6in |
| WING AREA | 718sq ft |
| EMPTY WEIGHT | 25,600lb |
| ALL-UP WEIGHT | 39,000lb |
| MAX SPEED | 360mph |
| CEILING | 26,000ft |
| RANGE | 2,000 miles |

*Right*: RH754, one of a few built as Brigand TF Mk Is from the first production batch of 80 aircraft delivered between January 1946 and February 1949. RH754 served with the A&AEE and de Havilland before being resigned to the ranges of the Proof & Experimental Establishment (P&EE) at Shoeburyness, Southend-on Sea.

*Below*: The first production-line Brigand was TF Mk 1, RH742, which enjoyed a lengthy career (for a Brigand), serving with the ECFS A&AEE and the ATDU. It was SOC on 17 June 1954.

# Type 170 Freighter and Wayfarer

## Development
A design that was developed during the closing stages of World War Two, the Type 170 had its roots in specifications 22/33 and C.9/45, which called for a rugged aircraft capable of transporting a standard British Army 3-ton truck. Although the original military adaptation was not taken up, chief designer, Archibald E Russell, saw the potential of the aircraft as a civilian short-range transport and so began the long story of the Freighter and Wayfarer.

## Design
Not the most elegant looking of aircraft, the Type 170 was a high-wing monoplane, with clam-shell nose doors, substantial fixed undercarriage and power provided by two Hercules sleeve-valve engines. The flight deck was positioned high above the cargo hold/cabin and was accessed via an internal ladder.

There were a wide range of Freighter and Wayfarer variants; the former, Mk I, retained the original clam-shell doors while the latter, Mk II, had a solid nose with a side entrance passenger access and loading door, plus the option of a reinforced floor for freight. The Freighters were employed solely for cargo operations while the Wayfarer, available in Mk II to Mk IIC variants, could carry up to 32 passengers.

Later versions of the Freighter included the Mk XI with a longer 108ft-span wing and extra fuel tanks; the Mk XIA mixed traffic variant; the Mk 21 with more power; the Mk 21E with 32 removable seats; Mk 31 with a bigger fin; Mk 31E, a convertible version of the Mk 31; Mk 31M military variant designed for supply drops and the 5ft-longer Mk 32 developed for Silver City Airways.

## Service
The prototype Freighter, G-AGPV, first flew on 2 December 1945 and was followed by the first 34-seat Wayfarer, G-AGVB on 30 April 1946. Service trials were carried out at Boscombe Down, Wiltshire, and proving flights in the colours of Channel Islands Airways.

After a successful world sales tour, early military orders were picked up for the Argentine Air Force and UK airlines began to see the potential of the Type 170, especially Silver City Airways. The airline adapted the Freighter to carry passengers and their cars and, 14 from July 1948, this service was carried out from Lympne to Le Touquet, northern France. Silver City also operated the Freighter 32, aka the 'Superfreighter', and even built a new airport, named 'Ferryfield' at Lydd, Kent, to operate the type on cross-Channel services from 1955. Silver City would also operate the 'Super-Wayfarer', which had a 60-passenger capacity.

The Type 170 was also operated by a large number of overseas airlines and air forces in the Royal New Zealand Air Force, which kept its Freighters in service until the early 1970s. In civilian hands, the type was also still abundant into the 1970s but numbers could be counted on one hand by the 1980s. The last flight by a Freighter was that of Mk 31M, CF-WAE (ex-RCAF), which was retired in 2004.

| Technical data – Type 170 Freighter Mk I-ID, IX, XIA, 21, 31 32 and Wayfarer Mk II, IIA-C | |
|---|---|
| ENGINE | (I, IA, II, IIA, IIB, IIC, XI and XIA) Two 1,675hp Bristol Hercules 632; (21, 21E and 21P) two 1,690hp Hercules 672; (31,31C, 31E, 31M and 32) two 1,980hp Hercules 734 |
| WINGSPAN | (I and II) 98ft; (XI, 21, 31 and 32) 108ft |
| LENGTH | (I, II, XI, 21 and 31) 68ft 4in; (32) 73ft 4in |
| HEIGHT | (I, II, XI, 21 and 31) 21ft 8in; (32) |
| WING AREA | (I and II) 1,405sq ft; (XI, 21, 31, and 32) 1,487sq ft |
| EMPTY WEIGHT | (I and II) 23,500lb; (IA) 24,000lb; (IIA and IIC) 25,500lb; (XI) 24,500lb; (XIA) 25,000lb; (21) 26,500lb; (21E) 28,000lb; (31) 27,000lb; (31E) 28,500lb; (32) 29,550lb |
| ALL-UP WEIGHT | (I and II) 36,500lb; (IA, IIA and IIC) 37,000lb; (XI and XIA) 39,000lb; (21 and 21E) 40,000lb; (31, 31E and 32) 44,000lb |
| MAX SPEED | (I, IA, II, IIA and IIC) 240mph; (XI and XIA) 195mph; (21, 21E, 31, 31E and 32) 225mph |
| CRUISING SPEED | (All marks) 163mph |
| CEILING | (I, IA, II, IIA and IIC) 22,000ft; (XI and XIA) 19,000ft; (21, 21E, 31, 31E and 32) 225mph |
| RANGE | (I, IA, II, IIA and IIC) 600 miles; (XI, XIA, 21 and 21E) 900 miles; (31, 31E and 32) 820 miles. |
| ACCOMMODATION | (I, II and XI) Three crew and 16 passengers; (IIA, 21E and 31E) three crew and 32 passengers; (IIC) three crew and 20 passengers; (21 and 31) two or three crew, 15 passengers and two cars or three crew and 52 passengers; (32) two crew and 23 passengers and three cars or three crew and 60 passengers |

Bristol Type 170 Freighter Mk 31M, G-BISU, was an ex-Royal New Zealand Air Force aircraft operated by Instone Air Line out of Stansted during the 1980s and early 1990s. Re-registered as C-FDFC, the aircraft was written off at Enstone, Oxfordshire, on 18 July 1996.

Named Valiant, G-ANVR, a Freighter Mk 32 first served with Air Charter.

# Type 171 and Sycamore

## Development
In the summer of 1944, Bristol formed a Helicopter Department at Filton with a rotorcraft design team led by Raoul Hafner. The Austrian-born designer, who was transferred from the Airborne Forces Experimental Establishment, drew on his pre-war experience with his own ARIII Gyroplane. The result was a four-seat, single-engine helicopter capable of both military and civilian operation under the designation Type 171.

## Design
Developed under the Ministry of Supply Specification E.20/45, the first two prototypes, designated Type 171 Mk 1 would be powered by American Pratt and Whitney Wasp Junior engines. The cabin section of the helicopter was made from light alloy while the tail-boom was stress-skinned. The latter was attached to a centrally mounted engine and gearbox with the rotor head driving three wooden monocoque blades.

## Service
The prototype, serialled VL958, was ready for engine testing in May 1947 and first flew on 27 July. The second machine, VL963, was in the air by February 1948 and it was this aircraft that became the first British helicopter to receive a Certificate of Airworthiness on 25 April 1949. Re-registered as G-ALOU, the second prototype appeared at that year's Paris Salon.

The third helicopter, the Type 171 Mk 2, was powered by an Alvis Leonides and first flew on 3 September 1949. The first production variant was the Type 171 Mk 3, which featured a shorter nose and a bigger cabin with room for three passengers in the rear. A Sycamore HC.10 and four HC.11 ambulance and communication machines were trialled by the Army Air Corps and four HC.12s were delivered to St Mawgan, Cornwall, for RAF trials in February 1952. Two Mk 3As were loaned to BEA, which had a freight hold behind the engine bay.

The Type 177 Mk 4 was the most prolific production variant and featured a taller landing gear and four cabin doors. HR.50, HC.51, Mk 14 and MK 52s were all sold overseas while the HR.13 and HR.14 were delivered to the RAF. These were employed on search and rescue duties, initially with 275 Squadron from April 1953. The RAF's Sycamores also served in Malaya, Cyprus and Borneo proving to be particularly adept at dropping troops into inhospitable regions.

## Production
In total, 181 Type 171s were built; two Mk 1s; one Mk 2; 23 Mk 3s and 3As (included two for BEA and four HR.12 for RAF) and 154 Mk 4s. Of the latter, three were built as HR.50, and seven HC.51s for the Royal Australian Navy; three Mk 14 for the Bangladesh Air Force; 50 Mk 52s for the German Air Force and Navy; two HR.13s and 82 HR.14s for the RAF.

## Type 171 and Sycamore

| Technical data – Type 171 Mk 1 and 2 and Mk 3, 3A, 4 (HC.10, HC.11, HR.12, HR.13, HR.14, HR.50, HC.51 and Mk 52) | |
|---|---|
| ENGINE | (Mk 1) One 450hp Pratt and Whitney Wasp Jr; (All others) one 550hp Alvis Leonides |
| ROTOR DIAMETER | (Mk 1) 47ft 3in; (All others) 48ft 7in |
| LENGTH | (Mk 1) 41ft 4in; (Mk 2) 41ft 6in; (All others) 48ft 7in |
| HEIGHT | (Mk 1, 2, 3 and 3A) 13ft 10; (Mk 4) 14ft 7in |
| EMPTY WEIGHT | (Mk 1) 3,800lb; (Mk 2) 3,770lb; (Mk 3 and 3A) 3,450lb; (Mk 4) 3,810lb |
| ALL-UP WEIGHT | (Mk 1) 4,850lb; (Mk 2) 5,200lb; (Mk 3, 3A and 4) 5,600lb |
| MAX CRUISING SPEED | 132mph |
| CRUISE RANGE | (Mk 1) 230 miles; (Mk 2) 300 miles; (Mk 3, 3A and 4) 330 miles |
| ACCOMMODATION | (Mk 1 and 2); (Mk 3, 3A and 4) 5 |

*Above left*: One of two Type 171 Mk 3As G-AMWG, named *Sir Gawain*, on passenger service duties between Birmingham and Gatwick in 1955.

*Above right*: The second prototype Type 171 Mk 1, G-ALOU after it became the first British helicopter to be issued with a Certificate of Airworthiness on 29 April 1949, in preparation for its appearance at the Paris Salon.

*Below left*: The sole Sycamore HC.10, WA578 was an ambulance variant and carried out operational trials in Malaya in 1949. Formerly accepted by the RAF on 14 August 1951, the aircraft served with the A&AEE until it was wrecked near Tidworth, Wiltshire, on 3 July 1956.

*Below right*: The first of just two Sycamore HR.13s was XD196 standardised with winches for ASR duties; it joined 275 Squadron at Linton-on-Ouse, North Yorkshire, on 13 April 1953.

# Type 167 Brabazon Mk 1

## Development
Chaired by Lord Brabazon of Tara, the well documented Inter-Departmental Committee, aka the 'Brabazon Committee', met in early 1943 to discuss the post-war civilian aviation needs in the UK. The resulting 'Brabazon Report' declared that five different airliner designs would be needed, beginning with the Type I for a large transatlantic airliner. The most prestigious of all the designs to emanate from the report, a contract to build a trans-oceanic aircraft was awarded to Bristol on 11 March 1943. Designated the Type 167 Brabazon Mk 1, it was hoped that the airliner would challenge the growing dominance of the USA in transport aircraft.

## Design
After much discussion and debate, the key ingredients of the new airliner such as size, capacity and performance were defined in Specification 2/44. This called for a 50-passenger capacity and a maximum take-off weight of 250,000lb.

By November 1944, the general layout of the Brabazon was determined; the fuselage alone was 16ft 9in in diameter and the giant airliner would be supported on the ground by a tricycle multi-wheel undercarriage. Power was to be provided by eight Centaurus radial engines coupled in pairs and driving contra-rotating propellers. The Brabazon Mk II, defined in Specification 2/46, was to be powered by four Proteus turboprops, a powerplant that would achieve success with the Britannia.

After the first drawings were released in April 1945, construction of the Brabazon Mk I commenced in November along with a new giant Assembly Hall and a new longer and stronger runway, which consumed a large proportion of the money that had already been spent on the project. The 177ft-long fuselage, wing centre section and tailplane were all constructed in one strong integral structure and on 4 October 1947, the huge airliner was moved to Filton's new assembly hall.

## Service
Rolled out in December 1948, the Brabazon Mk I, registered G-AGPW, carried out its maiden flight in the hands of chief test pilot Bill Pegg on 4 September 1949. On 14 June 1950, a restricted Certificate of Airworthiness was issued and the following day the aircraft flew to Heathrow, from where several demonstration flights were carried out. The rear of the aircraft was furnished with 30 BOAC reclinable seats for these demonstrations.

As with all prototypes, teething problems occurred, including fatigue cracks in the propeller mounting structure, which ended hopes of receiving a full Certificate of Airworthiness necessary for commercial passenger-carrying flights. A planned London to Nice flight for BEA with 180 passengers on board was curtailed and BOAC began to lose interest.

Up to 1952, the project had cost £3.4 million, and with no sign of orders from the airlines or the military, the government postponed work on the second Brabazon Mk II prototype. It was the prelude to the entire project being cancelled and was announced in the Commons on 17 July 1953.

After 164 flights and 382 flying hours, the Brabazon was scrapped, along with the incomplete Mk II, in October 1953. Bristol would benefit from the government's investment in the project with an improved infrastructure (included a new extended runway) and almost assured success with the Britannia.

## Type 167 Brabazon Mk 1

| Technical data – Type 167 Brabazon Mk 1 | |
|---|---|
| ENGINE | Eight 2,500hp Bristol Centaurus XX |
| SPAN | 230ft |
| LENGTH | 177ft |
| HEIGHT | 50ft |
| WING AREA | 5,317sq ft |
| EMPTY WEIGHT | 145,100lb |
| ALL-UP WEIGHT | 290,000lb |
| MAX SPEED | 300mph |
| CRUISING SPEED | 250mph |
| CRUISING ALTITUDE | 25,000ft |
| RANGE | 5,500 miles |
| ACCOMMODATION | 12 crew and 100 passengers |

*Right*: The Brabazon Mk I, G-AGWP, on final approach into London Airport on 16 June 1950. While located here, the airliner carried out a demonstration flights for dignitaries.

*Below*: One of the earliest views of the complete aircraft within the Assembly Hall in October 1947. Within a few years, this giant structure would be filled with the sound of Britannia production.

# Type 173 and Belvedere

## Development
Originally intended as a civilian transport helicopter, the story of the Type 173 would lead to military interest and a small order for the successful Type 192 Belvedere. A steep learning curve for the Bristol design team, the Type 173 drew heavily from lessons learned with the Type 171.

## Design
A pair of prototype Type 173 Mk 1s was built to Specification E.4/47, both featuring a pair of Sycamore rotor and control systems, each driven by an Alvis Leonides engine. The two engines were arranged to drive through a freewheel clutch while both gearboxes were connected by a single shaft; this meant that if one engine failed the second would continue to drive the rotors. The second prototype, Type 173 Mk 2, was fitted with a modified undercarriage and small stub wings at the front and rear. The third prototype only carried out hovering trials while the fourth and fifth never progressed beyond the engine-running stage. A naval version, designated Type 191, showed promise, but all three were used as ground test-rigs for the Gazelle engine, which would power the Type 192 Belvedere.

Designed for personnel and paratroop transportation and casualty evacuation, the Belvedere HC.1 was also capable of carrying large underslung loads. Early Belvederes had wooden rotor blades and anhedral tailplanes with end-plate fins. These were later updated to metal rotor blades, a compound anhedral tailplane plus powered controls, sliding doors, better air intakes and larger, low-pressure tyres.

## Service
The Type 173 Mk 1 was first hovered by CTD Hosegood on 3 January 1952 and flown for the first time from Filton on 24 August of that year. Registered as G-ALBN and later XF785, the helicopter was trialled by the RAF and Royal Navy on board HMS Eagle. The second prototype took to the air on 21 August 1953, followed by the Type 173 Mk 3, which only hovered on 9 November 1956.

The first Type 192 Belvedere HC.1 flew from Weston-super-Mare on 5 July 1958 and type clearance trials began at Boscombe Down in April 1960. The Belvedere HC.1 entered service at Odiham, Hampshire, with 66 Squadron in September 1961, 72 Squadron in November and 26 Squadron in June 1962. The type later saw extensive service overseas with 26 Squadron at Khormaksar, Yemen; and 66 Squadron at Seletar, Singapore; and Borneo; the latter during the Brunei campaign. The 26 Squadron lifted commandos from HMS *Centaur* into Tanganyika between January and March 1963 and again in the Radfan operations in Southern Arabia.

The Belvedere HC.1 was withdrawn from RAF service when 66 Squadron disbanded at Seletar on 17 March 1969.

## Production
One Type 173 Mk 1, 2, 3, 4 and 5 were built; three Type 191 Mk 1s and 26 Type 192 Belvedere HC.1s serialled XG447 to XG468 and XG473 to XG476. The latter were delivered between March 1959 and May 1962. By the latter date, the Bristol Helicopter Department had been taken over by Westland Aircraft Ltd.

| Technical data – Type 173/1-5, 191/1 and 192 Belvedere HC.1 | |
|---|---|
| ENGINE | (173/1 and 2) Two 550hp Alvis Leonides; (173/3–5 and 191/1) two 850hp Alvis Leonides Major; (192) two 1,465hp Napier Gazelle 2 |
| ROTOR DIAMETER | (173/1 and 2) 48ft 7in; (173/3–5) 48ft 9in; (192) 48ft 11in |
| LENGTH | (173/1 and 2) 55ft 2in; (173/3 and 4) 54ft 2in; (173/5 and 191/1) 50ft 3in; (192) 48ft 11in |
| HEIGHT | (173/1 and 2) 15ft; (173/3–5 and 192) 17ft; (191/1) |
| EMPTY WEIGHT | (173/1 and 2) 7,820lb; (173/3–5) 9,840lb; (191/1) 11,400lb; (192) 11,085lb |
| ALL-UP WEIGHT | (173/1) 10,600lb; (173/2) 11,000lb; (173/3-5) 13,500lb; (191/1) 17,000lb; (192) 19,000lb |
| MAX CRUISING SPEED | (192) 138mph; (All others) 115mph |
| CRUISE RANGE | (173/1 and 2) 185 miles; (173/3–5) 300 miles; (191/1) 500 miles; (192) 460 miles |
| ACCOMMODATION | (173/1 and 2); two crew and 13 passengers; (173/3–5) two crew and 14 passengers; (191/1) two crew and 16 passengers; (192) three crew and 18 passengers |

The second prototype, Type 173 Mk 2, G-AMJI with castoring front wheels and fixed rear wheels, being demonstrated at Farnborough. Note the stub wings fore and aft designed to take the load off the rotors and improve the cruising speed.

The first prototype Type 192 Belvedere HC.1, XG447 first flew from Weston-super-Mare on 5 July 1958. The aircraft was trialled by the A&AEE but never entered operational service.

# Britannia 100

## Development
It was fortuitous for Bristol that a BOAC MRE Requirement issued in 1946 coincided neatly with the Brabazon Committee Type III, Specification C.2/47 of April 1947. Bristol had already been awarded contracts for the Type I and III sections of the Brabazon report and the company's subsequent design for the Type 175 would suit BOAC's needs.

## Design
The Type 175 Britannia took shape under the leadership of Archibald E Russell and was initially to be powered by four Bristol Centaurus engines and carry 32–36 passengers. However, the Centaurus was found to be too powerful for the planned payload, so the design was modified to a 40–44 passenger layout which later rose to 42–48.

A pressurised low-wing monoplane, the fuselage was 12ft in diameter, coupled to a new, larger wing at 2,055sq ft and fitted with large double-slotted flaps. The original large Centaurus nacelles were reduced when the Proteus turboprop became available, while a substantial set of Messier main gear bogies uniquely retracted backwards to avoid the jet pipes.

Flying controls were unique for a civilian airliner of this size and included small servo tabs operated by the pilot, which moved the main control surfaces. Power was controlled equally and delicately by an Ultra electrically signalled engine control system. The Britannia was often jokingly referred to as 'just like any other aircraft, apart from the fact that the pilot's controls were not connected to the surfaces and the throttles were not connected to the engines'.

## Service
It was on 16 August 1952 that the prototype Britannia, G-ALBO (later designated Series 100) first flew from Filton with Bill Pegg at the controls. The flight was not without the odd uncomfortable moment for the crew, including one main undercarriage bogie that refused to lock down and smoke rising from the cabin floor. Despite this, the Britannia looked very promising and BOAC's pre-order of 25 aircraft, received on 28 July 1949, looked on course to be achieved by the planned date of 1954. Only a few external modifications were implemented, including extending and slightly upturning the wing tips and repositioning the jet pipes from the top of the nacelle to the trailing edges of the wings.

The Britannia was by then in a strong position and had the world market potentially at its feet. Compared to the Comet, which appeared, on paper at least, to be a very risky option, the Britannia was attracting delegations from the world's top airlines throughout 1953 and 1954.

Of the original BOAC order, only 15 Series 102s were built, the first of these carried out a series of demanding trials before the Britannia entered public service in February 1957 on the South African route. Subsequently, the Britannia took over BOAC services to Australia, Colombo, Hong Kong, Singapore and Tokyo. By December 1957, an average of 3,000 hours per aircraft had been reached, which rose to 3,750 hours by August 1958. The planned engine life of the Proteus was also encouraging; runs between overhauls at first were 1,600 hours but, by 1962, this had risen to 2,400 hours.

## Production
One Type 175 Britannia Mk I prototype was built, followed by two Series 101 prototypes and 15 production Series 102s for BOAC.

## Britannia 100

| Technical data – Britannia 100 series (101 and 102) | |
|---|---|
| ENGINE | (101) Four 2,800ehp Bristol Siddeley Proteus 625, four 3,780ehp Proteus 705, (combined) one 4,120ehp Proteus 755, two 3,900ehp Proteus 705 and one 5,500ehp Orion; (102) four 3,900ehp Proteus 705 |
| WINGSPAN | 142ft 3in |
| LENGTH | 114ft |
| HEIGHT | 36ft 8in |
| WING AREA | 2,075sq ft |
| EMPTY WEIGHT | 88,000lb |
| ALL-UP WEIGHT | 155,000lb |
| CRUISING SPEED | 362mph |
| RANGE | 3,450 miles with max payload |
| MAX RANGE | 4,580 miles |
| ACCOMMODATION | Seven crew and 61 passengers in 1st Class or 90 passengers in Coach (max) |
| CARGO SPACE | 665 cu/ft |

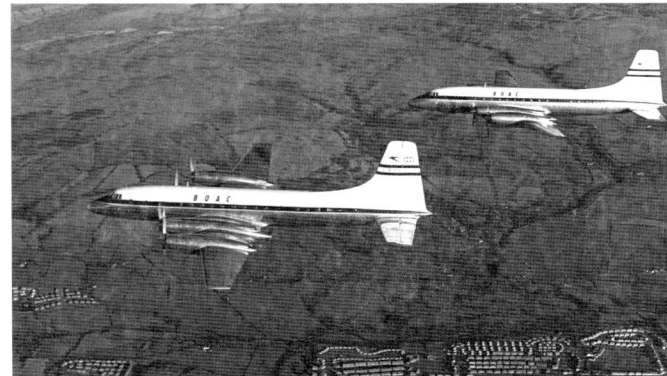

*Above left*: The first production Britannia 102, G-ANBA carried out full tropical trials for BOAC on the Johannesburg to Khartoum route and also established a maximum take-off weight of 150,000lb.

*Above right*: The first and second Britannia prototypes, G-ALBO (to rear) and G-ALRX in company. G-ALRX was lost on 4 February 1954 following reduction gear failure, being skilfully force landed on the mud of the Severn Estuary, Bristol, by test-pilot Arthur J 'Bill' Pegg.

*Below left*: Britannia 102, G-ANBK in BOAC markings; the airliner later served with Northeast Airlines and was broken up at Newcastle in March 1972.

*Below right*: Only 15 Series 102 Britannia's were built, including G-ANBB, which later served with Britannia Airways until it was written off at Ljubljana (Slovenia, former Yugoslavia) on 9 January 1966.

# Britannia 300

## Development
Before the prototype had flown, discussions with BOAC regarding a cargo version, or the Series 200, were being held. Before the first Series 200 took to the air, a stretched all-passenger variant was produced as the Series 300.

## Design
The series' predominant feature was its stretched fuselage (10ft 3in longer than the Series 100) and, from it, the new Series 300 was developed for passengers and the mixed passenger/freight Series 250. Capable of accommodating up to 133 passengers in tourist-class, the Series 300 could also cross the Atlantic non-stop, and this appealed to operators.

By 1955, the Series 310 had been introduced with a long-range capacity thanks to integral tanks in the outer wings, which increased capacity from 6,670 to 8,486 gals of fuel. The Proteus had now advanced to the Mk.755, which could develop 4,455ehp and this was more than enough for the increased gross weight of 185,000lb.

## Service
The first Series 300 aircraft was Britannia 301, G-ANCA, which first flew on 31 July 1956. BOAC placed an order for the Series 300, however the order was never delivered and was diverted to two 302s, which served Aeronaves de Mexico, two 305s to Transcontinental SA, two 307s to Air Charter and a single 309 to Ghana Airways.

BOAC decided that it wanted the Series 300LR (Long Range) instead. The single prototype, redesignated as the Series 311, first flew on 31 December 1956 and was registered as G-AOVA. BOAC subsequently took delivery of 18 production aircraft, Series 312, which were delivered to the airline from September 1957.

Following in El Al's footsteps, BOAC established services between London and New York in late 1957 and by 1959, was also flying across the Pacific to Tokyo. Canadian Pacific also received six Series 314s and a pair of Series 324s from April 1958, although the latter were in Cathay Pacific hands by 1961. Aircraft, such as the Series 302, which was initially ordered by BOAC, served Aeronaves de México and Ghana Airways instead. Four Series 318s saw sterling service with Cubana de Aviacion from 1958, including an interesting episode in support of Operation Carlota in 1975, when hundreds of Cuban soldiers were transported to Angola. Prior to this, Cubana leased one of its Britannias to Czechoslovak Airlines (CSA), so that this latest operator could establish its first scheduled transatlantic service from Prague to Havana from 1962 onwards. Cubana was the last major airline to fly the Britannia. The small fleet remained in service until 1990.

Affectionately known as the 'Whispering Giant' thanks to its quiet Proteus engines, the Britannia clearly could have made a bigger impact on the world airlines than it did. Even so, the airliner still managed to break at least three world air records, including the fastest crossing of the Atlantic and Pacific, plus the quickest time on the 'over-the-Pole' route. It was the world's first turboprop-powered large passenger airliner. During the period from 1957 to 1962, the world's Britannia fleet managed to cover 222 million miles and carry more than three million passengers. At that time, a Britannia is said to have carried out a take-off at some point around the globe every 13 minutes.

## Production

Thirty-two aircraft were built in three major series: Series 300: one 301, two 302s, two 305s, two 307Fs, two 308s, one 309; Series 310: 11 312s, two 312Fs, three 313s and four 314s and Series 320: two 324.

| Technical data – Britannia 300 series (301, 302, 306-309, 311–319 and 324) | |
|---|---|
| ENGINE | (101) Four 4,120/4,450ehp Bristol Siddeley Proteus 755, 756, 757, 761 or 765 |
| WINGSPAN | 142ft 3in |
| LENGTH | 124ft 3in |
| HEIGHT | 37ft 6in |
| WING AREA | 2,075sq ft |
| EMPTY WEIGHT | (301, 302) 92,500lb; (306–309) 90,000lb; (311–319) 82,537lb; (324) 86,400lb |
| ALL-UP WEIGHT | 185,000lb |
| CRUISING SPEED | 357mph |
| RANGE (Max Payload) | (301, 302) 3,450 miles; (All others) 4,268 miles |
| MAX RANGE | (301, 302) 4,440 miles; (306–309) 5,334 miles; (311–319) 5,310 miles; (324) 5,340 miles |
| ACCOMMODATION | (301, 302) Four–seven crew and 73 passengers in 1st Class or 139 passengers in Coach (max); (All others) Four–seven crew and 82 passengers in 1st Class or 139 passengers in Coach (max) |
| CARGO SPACE | (306–309) 845 cu/ft; (All others) 900 cu/ft |

*Right*: The sole prototype Series 311, G-AOVA, first flew on 31 December 1956 but was not accepted by BOAC because of the wear and tear it had sustained during development flying.

*Below*: Britannia 305, G-ANCD, in the temporary livery of Compania Cubana de Aviacón at the start of a 27,400-mile-long sales tour of Spain, Portugal, Cuba and South America in 1958.

# Britannia C Mk 1 and C Mk 2

## Development
The Ministry of Supply placed an order for three mixed-traffic Britannia's in February 1955, designated Series 252, for leasing to charter operators. Built at Belfast, these aircraft, registered G-APPE, G-APPF and G-APPG would later form part of a more substantial order for the RAF under the designation Series 253. This decision was made following the cancellation of the Vickers V1000 turbojet transport in 1955.

## Design
In RAF service, the Series 252 was designated the Britannia C Mk2 and the Series 253, the C Mk1. Both series featured more powerful Proteus 255 engines, a metal floor the full length of the cabin and fittings for rear-facing seats, stretchers or cargo plus a cockpit furnished with full military instrumentation and radio aids.

## Service
The RAF ordered six Britannias in January 1956 and increased the number to 23 aircraft by the end of the year. The prototype C.1, XL635, later named Bellatrix, first flew from Sydenham on 29 December 1958. Two of the Ex-Ministry of Supply Series 252s, now designated the Britannia C Mk 2, XN598 Altair and XV404 Canopus were delivered to the RAF Transport Command for crew training on 19 March and 8 April 1959, respectively. These aircraft were attached to 99 Squadron at Lyneham. Also based at Lyneham, 511 Squadron received its first Britannia in December 1959, but in reality all aircraft were pooled as 99/511 Squadron.

  RAF Britannias served all four corners of the globe with ease and were often called upon to provide aid in remote areas, such as Belize following Hurricane Hattie in November 1961. Six aircraft from 99 and 511 squadrons delivered medical teams and supplies to the country and evacuated the families of government personnel. Another notable achievement was the longest non-stop flight by an RAF Britannia. The commanding officer of 511 Squadron flew his aircraft from Palisadoes Airport, Jamaica, to St Mawgan, Cornwall, in 12 hours 40 minutes, a distance of 4,160 miles.

  The familiar story of government defence cuts brought about their early departure from service in January 1976. However, one military aircraft, Series 312F XX367, remained with the A&AEE until 1984, having previously served with BOAC as G-AOVM, followed by Air Spain as EC-BSY. XX367 was sold on to Business Cash Flow (BCF) Aviation in Zaire where it continued to operate until 1994. However, one Britannia, which beat them all, namely the only complete ex-RAF Britannia C Mk 1 XM496 Regulus, which entered service on 17 September 1960. After being withdrawn in 1975, the Britannia went on to serve with several airlines, including Monarch, finally seeing out its flying days as EL-WXA with Transair Cargo in August 1997. The world's last airworthy Britannia was flown into Kemble, where it is proudly displayed today in its original RAF colours thanks to the Britannia XM496 Preservation Society.

## Production

In total, 20 Britannia C Mk 1s, serialled XL635 to XL640 and XL657 to XL660, XM489 to XM491, XM496 to XM498 and XM517 to XM519 were built by Short Brothers and Harland, Belfast and delivered between May 1959 and December 1960. Three C.2s, serialled XN392 (ex-G-APPE), XN398 (ex-G-APPF) and XV404 (ex-G-APPG) were also produced.

| Technical data – Britannia C Mk 1 and C Mk 2 (Series 252 and 253) | |
|---|---|
| ENGINE | Four 4,445ehp Bristol Siddeley Proteus 755 |
| WINGSPAN | 142ft 3in |
| LENGTH | 124ft 3in |
| HEIGHT | 37ft 6in |
| WING AREA | 2,075sq ft |
| EMPTY WEIGHT | (252) 90,500lb; (253) 90,600lb |
| LOADED (MAX) | 185,000lb |
| CRUISING SPEED | (252) 355mph; (253) 360mph |
| RANGE | 4,268 miles with max payload |
| MAX RANGE | 5,334 miles |
| CREW | Four to six crew and 139 passengers |
| CARGO SPACE | (252) 5,850sq ft; (253) 6,120sq ft |

Britannia C.1, XL636, *Argo* of 99/511 Squadron (the units' aircraft were pooled), the second of 20 C.1s delivered to the RAF, the aircraft was sold on 6 May 1976 and registered OO-YCE.

The third of three Series 252 Britannias, designated C.2, was XN404 *Canopus* and was sold onto the civilian market on 17 December 1975. Despite their high airframe hours, every ex-RAF Britannia continued to serve smaller airliners in Africa, Europe and the Middle East.

# Type 188

## Development
The Type 188 had its roots in Operational Requirement (OR) 330, which would lead to the demise of Avro 730. A test vehicle would be needed for high-speed flight, which led to OR.134T issued in February 1953 calling for an aircraft capable of at least Mach 2 (twice the speed of sound). Against a great deal of competition, Bristol won a contract for six aircraft – later reduced to three – only two of which would fly. Following the cancellation of the Avro 730 in 1957, the expected same fate never took place for the Bristol design and the project continued as a high-speed research machine with the potential to influence the future Concorde.

## Design
The Type 188 was designed to investigate the effects of kinetic heating of airframes at speeds of Mach 2. As a result, the aircraft had to be manufactured from special steels joined together with a 'puddle welding' technique instead of riveting. Another feature unique to the Type 188 was a fused-quartz windscreen and canopy. In order to reach twice the speed of sound, a pair of Rolls-Royce RA.24R engines would be needed, but, the Type 188 would have to settle for a pair of Gyron Junior DGJ.10 engines instead with a variable-geometry intake system.

## Service
The first of two prototypes, serialled XF923, was rolled out at Filton on 26 April 1961. Following a comprehensive set of pre-flight tests and engine runs, which revealed a problem with intake design, the Type 188 began taxying trials in February 1962. Poor weather delayed the maiden flight until 14 April 1962 when Bristol chief test pilot, Godfrey L Auty, took off for a 23-minute flight direct to Boscombe Down. After appearing at the SBAC in September, XF923 returned to Filton following the completion of its initial test programme.

The second Type 188, XF926, first flew on 29 April 1963, by which time it was realised that the aircraft fell far short of performance expectations. Handed over to RAE Bedford, XF926 carried out 51 flights but could only manage a maximum speed of Mach 1.88 at 36,000ft and endurance was pitifully low. XF926 made its last flight on 12 January 1964, bringing to an end a project that cost the British taxpayer £20 million. Both XF923 and XF926 were sent to PEE Shoeburyness in April 1966, but the latter survived after it was recovered in 1972 and was sent to Cosford, Shropshire, for restoration.

| Technical data – Type 188 | |
|---|---|
| ENGINE | Two 14,000lb de Havilland Gyron Junior DGJ.10 turbojets |
| WINGSPAN | 35ft 1in |
| LENGTH | 71ft |
| HEIGHT | 13ft 4in |
| WING AREA | 396sq ft |
| EMPTY WEIGHT | 28,000lb |
| MAX TAKE-OFF | 37,527lb |
| MAX SPEED | Mach 1.88 at 36,000ft |

Bristol Type 188 XF923 at Boscombe Down in 1962 after it was delivered from Filton in April.

Despite being cancelled in 1964, the Type 188 did contribute to the design of Concorde especially with regard to the use of stainless steel. As a result, Concorde was constructed of conventional aluminium alloys. Data from the Gyron Junior also contributed to the developed of the supersonic airliners Olympus engines.

# Other books you might like:

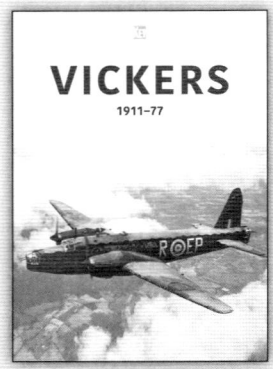
Aviation Industry Series, Vol. 4

Aviation Industry Series, Vol. 3

Aviation Industry Series, Vol. 2

Aviation Industry Series, Vol. 1

Historic Military Aircraft Series, Vol. 22

For our full range of titles please visit:
**shop.keypublishing.com/books**

---

# VIP Book Club
## Sign up today and receive
# TWO FREE E-BOOKS

Be the first to find out about our forthcoming book releases and receive exclusive offers.

Register now at **keypublishing.com/vip-book-club**

Our VIP Book Club is a 100% spam-free zone, and we will never share your email with anyone else. You can read our full privacy policy at: privacy.keypublishing.com